Praise for *Delivering the WOW*

"Richard Fain didn't just build ships—he built a culture of excellence that transformed an entire industry. Having worked alongside him for over two decades on Royal Caribbean's board, I witnessed firsthand how his extraordinary leadership combined visionary strategy with masterful execution. Richard possessed that rare ability to see where the market was heading before anyone else, then align an entire organization around that North Star with remarkable clarity of purpose. Richard's insights on building transformational culture and maintaining unwavering commitment to long-term vision offer invaluable lessons for leaders in any industry. Simply put, Richard Fain was one of the finest CEOs I've ever had the privilege to work with."

—**Tom Pritzker,** executive chairman of Hyatt Hotels

"Considering I've seen it all in 40+ years in the cruise industry, I was genuinely surprised by how many of Richard Fain's behind-the-scenes stories had me saying, 'Wow, I had no idea!' The book strikes that rare balance between useful lessons and stirring emotions . . . In this inspiring book, Richard proves that with the right vision, culture, and resilience, anyone can emerge from any challenge bigger, bolder, and better than ever."

—**Michelle Fee,** founder and CEO of Cruise Planners
(the largest home-based travel network in the US)

"This book is more than a business story—it's a guide to building a culture rooted in purpose, passion, and lasting impact. It's about achievement that goes beyond the bottom line and a journey marked by bold decisions, deep care for people, and a commitment to leaving things better than he found them. By sharing his lessons, Richard has given every reader a rare gift: a blueprint for leading with heart, sustaining excellence, and transforming challenges into enduring legacy."

—**Don Thompson,** former CEO, McDonald's Corporation

"Some management books sink readers with ungrounded theory and simplistic bromides. By contrast, Richard Fain's new book *Delivering the WOW* also delivers the "how" with the wow. He describes his triumphs in elevating the standards of excellence in the customer experience of travelers and so much more. This book shows how a great leader . . . piloted the operational, marketing, financial, strategic, and staffing transformation of the cruise industry. With 35 years at the helm of Royal Caribbean, Richard shares fascinating candid, personal explanations to show that the destinations they reached as an enterprise did not happen by putting leadership on cruise control. The entire travel sector learned from Royal Caribbean's innovation. Richard offers a library of wise maxims to guide future leaders across industries, across sectors, across oceans, and across continents."

—**Jeffrey A. Sonnenfeld,** senior associate dean for leadership studies, Yale School of Management

Culture *as* Catalyst *for* Lasting Success

DELIVERING
the
WOW

RICHARD FAIN
Chairman and former CEO of Royal Caribbean Group

FAST
COMPANY
Press

This publication is designed to provide accurate and authoritative information in regard to the subject matter covered. It is sold with the understanding that the publisher and author are not engaged in rendering legal, accounting, or other professional services. Nothing herein shall create an attorney-client relationship, and nothing herein shall constitute legal advice or a solicitation to offer legal advice. If legal advice or other expert assistance is required, the services of a competent professional should be sought.

Fast Company Press
New York, New York
www.fastcompanypress.com

Copyright © Deliver the Wow, LLC

All rights reserved.

Thank you for purchasing an authorized edition of this book and for complying with copyright law. No part of this book may be reproduced, stored in a retrieval system, used for training artificial intelligence technologies or systems, or transmitted by any means, electronic, mechanical, photocopying, recording, or otherwise, without written permission from the copyright holder.

This work is being published under the Fast Company Press imprint by an exclusive arrangement with Fast Company. Fast Company and the Fast Company logo are registered trademarks of Mansueto Ventures, LLC. The Fast Company Press logo is a wholly owned trademark of Mansueto Ventures, LLC.

Distributed by Greenleaf Book Group

For ordering information or special discounts for bulk purchases, please contact Greenleaf Book Group at PO Box 91869, Austin, TX 78709, 512.891.6100.

Design and composition by Greenleaf Book Group
Cover design by Greenleaf Book Group
Photos courtesy of Royal Caribbean Group and Helen Stephan.

Publisher's Cataloging-in-Publication data is available.

Print ISBN: 978-1-63908-159-2

eBook ISBN: 978-1-63908-160-8

Audiobook ISBN: 978-1-63908-161-5

In 1999, the author established the Fain Scholarship Fund to support the education of Royal Caribbean Group employees and their children. Since its inception, the author has been the sole contributor to the fund, which currently provides an average of $200,000 in annual support. All of the author's proceeds from this book will be donated to the scholarship program.

To offset the number of trees consumed in the printing of our books,
Greenleaf donates a portion of the proceeds from each printing to the Arbor Day Foundation. Greenleaf Book Group has replaced over 50,000 trees since 2007.

Printed in the United States of America on acid-free paper

25 26 27 28 29 30 31 32   10 9 8 7 6 5 4 3 2 1

First Edition

To Colleen,

My *sine qua non* (without which nothing).

To the people of Royal Caribbean Group,

your passion,

your creativity,

your commitment to excellence

give these stories their soul.

Contents

Introduction 1

Chapter 1 Bigger, Bolder, Better 5

Chapter 2 "Good Enough" Isn't Good Enough 23

Chapter 3 A 40-Day Countdown to an Uncertain Future 51

Chapter 4 Grow or Die 63

Chapter 5 It's the People, It's the People, It's the People 83

Chapter 6 What the Hell?! 107

Chapter 7 Innovation in Ship Design 127

Chapter 8 Innovation Beyond Ship Design 163

Chapter 9 COVID—The End of Cruising? 185

Chapter 10 Passing the Torch 203

Acknowledgments 209

Glossary 211

About the Author 215

Scuttlebutt:

Scuttlebutt comes from the verb *to scuttle,* meaning "to cut a hole," and the noun *butt,* meaning "cask." In the 1800s, the *scuttlebutt* was a cask containing a ship's daily supply of fresh water with a hole for access. Sailors would stand around the scuttlebutt and exchange gossip—the original water cooler.

Introduction

"**WOW!**" That's the word on everyone's lips as we walk around *Icon of the Seas*, the world's largest and most spectacular cruise ship.

The date is November 27, 2023, and I am here in Turku, Finland, about to participate in the ceremony transferring the ship's ownership from the shipyard that built *Icon* to Royal Caribbean. During the ceremony, we will officially accept delivery and pay the final installment of the $2 billion investment. The head of the Finnish shipyard will order the yard's flags to be lowered, and Captain Henrik will order the ship's flags to be raised.

WOWs are more than spontaneous reflexes. They are rallying cries, and they have the power to mobilize a workforce to achieve the unthinkable. They may be hard to earn, but they are worth their weight in gold. They're our company's reason for being.

I didn't yet appreciate any of this when I first started working at one of Royal Caribbean's shareholding companies in 1975. Back then, I thought that doing my job with enthusiasm and imagination was enough. I never appreciated the importance of culture and could not have imagined its power as a catalyst for transformational growth.

To put this in perspective, our three original ships combined couldn't have carried the crew of *Icon of the Seas*, let alone its guests. Today, *Icon* will be our 65th ship, and Royal Caribbean is on track to reach a market value greater than all our competitors in the cruise industry combined.

After having the privilege to lead this wonderful company for over 33 years as chairman and CEO, I can see clearly that it is a strong and forward-looking culture that has driven our success. There is simply no force that matches the power of passionate people working together toward a common goal—a North Star.

Twenty-five years ago, we formalized the use of the term WOW by accident. We were brainstorming to create an acronym that would capture the core values we wanted our people to embrace. We wanted to call the program GOLD, but we struggled to find a word beginning with D to complete the acronym. Finally, someone suggested "Deliver the WOW," and we all gasped. It so perfectly captured what made our vacations so special. It just felt right.

Today, standing aboard *Icon*, my heart is overwhelmed. This ship is not just steel and design; she's a living, breathing testament to what passion, insatiability, and shared purpose can achieve. Every step I take across these decks, every smile I see from the extraordinary team who brought her to life, fills me with awe and gratitude. And yet, as magnificent as she is, I know this moment is only a single chapter in a much greater journey.

The culture is our most important and enduring legacy.

The true story lives in the moments—the joy, the pride, the challenges, and the unwavering belief that we could always aim higher, do better, and dream bigger. The ship may be the most visible expression of that journey, but the culture—built by countless hearts and hands—is its most important and enduring legacy. It has been a profound privilege to be part of it all, at the very heart of one of the most dynamic, ever evolving, and truly magical industries in the world.

Along the way, I've learned some valuable lessons that I believe could be helpful to the next generation of leaders in any industry or association. I also love stories and scuttlebutt, and I'm eager to share both with fellow cruise aficionados and our own employees.

In this book, I recount the highs and lows: the triumphs, the setbacks, and the black swan events that nearly brought us to our knees. It's the story of a small cruise company that innovated and grew to become a global powerhouse by methodically building a WOW culture that every employee proudly lives every day.

I'll focus on several principles that I believe were particularly meaningful—such as alignment, intentionality, continuous improvement, and more. I'll explore them in the context of unforgettable moments I encountered in an industry full of surprises, adventures, and lessons.

I've been incredibly fortunate. Royal Caribbean was founded on a vision of innovation, and the women and men I work with here are some of the most caring, dedicated, and passionate people in the world. I'm in awe of them, and this is really their story.

Bon voyage.

Shipshape:

The original phrase *shipshape and Bristol fashion* referred to a ship built and maintained to exceptionally high standards. Bristol was a British harbor known for its difficult port conditions with tidal variations of 30 feet or more. Vessels that could handle such challenges were highly regarded, and that tradition of excellence has carried over into the modern use of the term *shipshape*.

Bigger, Bolder, Better

When I first heard of Royal Caribbean Cruise Lines in the mid-1970s, it was a small Norwegian company with three 720-passenger ships and a solid reputation for excellence. I learned about it as part of my new job as treasurer of Gotaas-Larsen Shipping Corporation. Gotaas-Larsen was a part owner of Royal Caribbean, but when I joined the company, Royal Caribbean wasn't even mentioned. It was only after I had been there for some months that I discovered that Gotaas-Larsen owned a third of this small but successful cruise business.

Unfortunately, I was also told that I would have nothing to do with the cruise line and that I should focus solely on solving the problems of the big shipping company. Bummer. The cruise industry sounded interesting, and it was disappointing that I would not be involved.

The good news, for me, was that at 28 years of age, I was now an officer of a large international shipping company. The bad news was that the company was virtually bankrupt and sinking fast.

Gotaas-Larsen operated a large fleet of ships including oil tankers, liquified natural gas carriers, dry cargo vessels, and drilling rigs. It had once been very profitable, but it was now in serious financial trouble. The 1973–1974 oil embargo had devastated the shipping business, and Gotaas-Larsen had placed orders for a series of ships it had no money to pay for. As treasurer, my job—my only job—was to raise the financial capital to right this sinking ship. Unfortunately, our ownership of a minority interest in Royal Caribbean was not going to be helpful in that regard.

One day, Kenneth Trippe, the president of Gotaas-Larsen, came to see me with a new assignment. Ken was a tall, handsome leader with a strong financial background. He had taken a chance on this young financial analyst and invited me to join Gotaas-Larsen. At this formative stage of my career, Ken mentored me and taught me to focus attention on the areas that mattered most. To my surprise, he now assigned me to analyze a proposal from Royal Caribbean.

Ken explained that Ed Stephan, the cruise line's founder and president, had made a proposal that sounded not only radical but also downright bizarre. Royal's three ships each carried 720 guests, but Ed wanted to enlarge the first of these ships, *Song of Norway*, so that she could carry 1,040 guests. To do so, Ed proposed to cut the ship in half, build a new, longer midsection filled with cabins, float out the bow of the ship, float in the new midsection, float the bow back in, and—finally—glue the pieces back together again.

At the time, it sounded impossible—actually, to me, it still does—but the engineers said it would work, and Ed Stephan was a man who inspired confidence. Thin and distinguished looking, he had served as an artillery officer in Korea, earning two bronze stars, and he carried himself with military bearing. He had already helped transform the industry with his vision of modern, purpose-built cruise ships dedicated to warmwater cruising, so we had faith that he could do even more. Ken's comment was that "As desperate as we are for cash, we have to consider seriously any proposal Ed puts forward."

The economics of the idea were compelling. Inserting a new 85-foot midsection would add 45 percent to the capacity of the ship (and to her revenue) but would only increase operating costs by 20 percent. The net result would be a larger ship with better economies of scale. On the surface, his idea was sheer craziness, but financially, this bizarre plan was a thing of beauty.

The difficulty for Gotaas-Larsen was that the project would interrupt the revenue from the vessel for several months while the ship was being lengthened. For a company in serious financial difficulty, doing a project that affected cash flow was a tough pill to swallow.

Ken asked me to give him an analysis of whether we should agree to this proposal. It was then that I learned that Royal Caribbean was a partnership of three equal owners: Gotaas-Larsen and two Norwegian companies, Anders Wilhelmsen & Co., and IM Skaugen & Co. I also learned that all decisions had to be unanimous, which meant that Gotaas-Larsen could veto the proposal.

Ken and I discussed the plan at length, and he decided that the long-term advantages of lengthening the *Song of Norway* outweighed the short-term pain it would cause. In retrospect, this experience was a precursor to the kind of decision we would face so often at Royal

The *Song of Norway* in the middle of its conversion,
when the two halves of the ship were separated.

The back half of the Song of Norway waits to be reconnected to the rest of the ship after the new mid-body was inserted.

Ed Stephan with a model of *Song of Norway*.

Caribbean: Should we suffer a large short-term cost (in this case, the loss of immediate cash flow) for a likely but uncertain improvement in our long-term future?

The work was completed on time and on budget, and the rebuilt ship operated smoothly and well. I had been genuinely confounded by the complexity of the engineering and amazed by how calm and confident all the technical people were. But their confidence was justified. In the end, it worked exactly as planned, and there were no technical surprises. Whew! The longer ship was truly shipshape.

> **Should we suffer a short-term cost for an expected but uncertain improvement in our long-term future?**

When we surveyed our repeat guests to see how they liked the ship's new look and feel, about one-third of the guests thought it was better; a third thought it was worse; and one-third didn't notice any difference. So, we had increased our revenue, and two-thirds of our guests were either satisfied or better with the change. Taking a risk on the lengthening proved to be a home run decision.

After that success, Ed Stephan returned with more proposals. He suggested lengthening a second ship, *Nordic Prince*. And then he proposed building a fourth ship, *Song of America*. All these proposals were unanimously approved, and all were successes.

During this period, I received several promotions at Gotaas-Larsen, and in 1981, when Ken Trippe stepped down, I became copresident with Alf Clausen. Alf was a gifted engineer who had started as technical director and later oversaw all the operating and technical activities of the company. On the surface, Alf and I couldn't have been more different. He was Norwegian, and I was American. He loved gardening, and I loved gadgets. He had spent his entire career in shipping, and I had spent mine doing finance for different industries.

Nevertheless, we formed a remarkably strong partnership. Alf was pragmatic and focused. I don't know whether he taught me more about engineering or I taught him more about finance, but the combination worked well and was especially valuable during those dark days in the shipping industry.

During this same period, I became more involved with Royal Caribbean, and eventually, Alf and I joined the cruise line's six-man board. (Note to present-day readers: At that time, it was a *six-man board*, not a *six-person board*.) I was honored to have this position, especially at the age of 34.

The Norwegian partners always treated me graciously, but they couldn't hide that they considered it a bit strange to have such a youngster involved. I grew a mustache in the hope that it would make me look older. It didn't help.

A BOLD PROPOSAL

After the success of his earlier proposals, Ed Stephan presented a new and even more ambitious idea. This time, he recommended a fifth ship for the fleet, the biggest yet. The idea was to use the base of *Song of America*, add a new fire zone to the length of the ship, and add a new deck to the height of the ship. This would create space for 1,800 guests, more than any other purpose-built cruise ship and with even greater economies of scale.

This latest proposal sparked a vigorous discussion with the board. The new ship would, by itself, increase Royal Caribbean's capacity by more than 40 percent. Where would all that demand come from? And the size—no one had ever contemplated such a large cruise ship before. The ship wouldn't just be large physically; it would be a huge bet on the company's future.

The two Norwegian owners had diametrically opposing views. Arne Wilhelmsen strongly supported the idea. He believed that the industry would continue to grow and emphasized the importance of increasing Royal Caribbean's market share. Morits Skaugen was more cautious.

He was worried about overbuilding and kept quoting the adage "Trees don't grow to heaven," meaning that things have a natural limit.

Ed was a powerful advocate for his bold idea, in part due to his persuasive combination of passion and military restraint. Ed remained adamant that we couldn't afford to miss this opportunity, and he grew increasingly frustrated by the impasse between the two Norwegian partners. No one outright said, "You're wrong; it's a bad idea," but neither could the partners reach a mutually acceptable decision. Finally, they agreed to create a steering committee to study the idea.

To my surprise, Arne and Morits asked me to chair it.

I think they asked me because they saw me as independent. I had not sided with either of them or expressed a view on the proposal. Ironically, the reason I hadn't yet taken a position wasn't to be careful or politically neutral. The simple truth was that I didn't feel I knew enough to have a considered opinion.

At the time, being asked to lead this project was exciting, but a bit scary. I was honored to be appointed, but couldn't help but feel that I had just been handed a "poisoned chalice"—tasked with an impossible challenge.

Looking back, this confusing period feels like a turning point—one of those moments that later reveals itself as pivotal. What none of us realized at the time was that this committee wouldn't just determine the fate of a ship. It would help redefine our company's strategy, reshape our approach to design, and even ignite a culture that would drive innovation and growth.

GETTING STARTED

It was immediately clear that we would need a very different approach to this topic. All the previous big decisions—the ship lengthenings, the new ship order, etc.—had been based on incremental change. Each case involved continuing to operate as we always had and just making the operation a bit larger. In each of those projects, the short-term economics were so powerful that a simple financial analysis made those decisions easy. But this proposal was different. The cost of ships had risen, our competitors were building more aggressively, and the size of ships was becoming a critical factor.

For this decision, we needed to approach the question with intentionality: a focused and disciplined mindset to ensure that every step aligned with our longer-term goal—our North Star. There could be no shortcuts, no superficial PowerPoint analysis. True intentionality requires an unwavering focus on the longer-term objective and not being distracted by easy compromises.

> **True intentionality requires an unwavering focus on the longer-term objective and not being distracted by easy compromises.**

We quickly decided that our first meeting would not focus on the project itself but on *how* we would work together. We met in a conference room in Wilhelmsen's offices in Oslo. They offered a large conference room, but I preferred their smaller one because I hoped it would make the conversation more intimate. Amid much grumbling, we met for an entire day but banned any discussion of the project itself. We wanted to concentrate on our collaborative approach and shared goals. It was a long and rambling discussion, and through it, the committee members began to get comfortable with one another.

By the end of that day, we hadn't solved a single technical issue, but we had built something much more important: trust and a sense of shared purpose. We knew that was the real foundation for everything we were about to tackle.

Today, the business world has grown more task oriented. We define a goal and pursue it with laser-focused efficiency. Zoom meetings rush directly at a problem, with the participants defending their point of view. An all-day meeting just to get oriented and start to know each other was unusual in the 1980s, and it is almost unthinkable today.

But our goal was to make sure we addressed the issue in depth, not to reach an acceptable compromise. True collaboration is messy and inefficient. It requires people to interrupt each other, get frustrated, and sigh and roll their eyes and yet continue to get along, listen, and think issues through together. Real collaboration runs on passion, but it is hard to express passion to a tiny face in a little box on a computer screen. Emojis lack the impact of a finger in the air. True collaboration leads to far better outcomes, so it is worth the extra time.

CLEARER VISION

Ed Stephan and I quickly realized that the committee needed help to conduct its research and to articulate its views to a skeptical board. An outside third party could provide data more quickly and could help us refine our vision of how the industry was evolving. In the end, we hired consultants from Arthur D. Little.

Some businesspeople make fun of consultants, saying they only tell you what you already know. There's an old joke that a consultant is someone who borrows your watch and then tells you the time. Others view consultants as the geniuses you hire to give you The Ultimate Answer. Neither approach works. Outsiders will never know as much as the people who do the work.

My experience with consultants is that the results are always at the extremes. Either they are extremely helpful or not at all. One way they help is by eliciting the information buried deep within an organization. Arthur D. Little spent a lot of time talking to our people and sussing out their thoughts. They also forced us to sit down and focus on questions that would normally get pushed aside by the day-to-day priorities of running a business.

Through these conversations, we developed a clearer understanding of our industry and our place within it. Traditionally, our cruises had been especially appealing to well-to-do, older guests, often retired, or to newlyweds with the time and money for a honeymoon. One of our most evocative early ads captured this image. It showed a couple in evening attire toasting each other with fine crystal and candlelight—in a rowboat. The caption read, *Now Imagine The Same Idea, On A Slightly Larger Scale*. It was wonderfully clever and attention-getting, but it reinforced a narrow view of cruises as places primarily for wealthy people with no children.

As our work proceeded, it also became clear that we risked being seduced by our own success. Our guests were more than satisfied with our product; they were thrilled. People who returned from a cruise vacation didn't just say they had a good time; they became evangelists about a transformative experience. But enthusiasm from existing customers wasn't enough; we needed to find a way to excite our base without sacrificing the larger opportunity ahead.

Our explicit focus on broadening our markets helped. Every time someone in a meeting pointed out how much our existing cruises were loved, we reminded each other to redirect the conversation back to the goal of a more exciting future.

An early Royal Caribbean ad reinforcing the image of cruising as elegant and passive.

SAYING NO TO INCREMENTALISM

Our original three-month deadline came and went. The committee continued to learn and argue through six months of research and debate, and finally, we reached a conclusion, becoming aligned in the way that only people who have puzzled and disagreed and reached insight together can.

Not only was the cruise market growing fast enough to absorb a new, larger ship, but the industry was also at an inflection point. Cruising was poised to transform from a niche industry aimed at a small segment of the American public to a nationwide obsession with far broader appeal. There had already been efforts to expand this audience by some in the industry—Carnival with its "Fun Ships" campaign, for example, and Princess with its *Love Boat* tie-in—but we hadn't yet cracked the code.

So, absolutely, we concluded that we should build this new ship. And, absolutely, there would be plenty of demand to fill it. But we had an opportunity to do so much more. We could help transform the industry and give people who had never considered cruising something better that was worth their time and their money.

We also identified a danger. If we didn't build this ship, Royal Caribbean risked being stuck in the middle—a company too large to succeed as a niche operator but still too small to afford the kind of marketing and product innovations needed to stay competitive. We could be niche or national, but if we tried to stay in the middle, we would be crushed.

The key conclusion from our analysis wasn't just that more people would buy cruises; it was that more people would buy our cruises *if we gave them something better to buy*. Specifically, our research showed that people wanted more choice in every aspect of their vacations—choices about what to eat, how to be entertained, and which activities would enrich their days.

To be successful, it wasn't enough just to refocus our marketing efforts. We would need to adjust our product offering to reflect the broader desires of this new and larger market. If people wanted variety, we needed to offer more activities, which meant more spaces on the ship with different things to do. If the family market was to become a key market segment for us, we needed to offer more activities geared to a younger audience, with spaces designed for both the children and their parents. If we were going to appeal to a broader demographic, we needed to offer much more variety in the choice of staterooms, restaurants, and bars.

All these new initiatives wouldn't fit in the traditional envelope. It required an even bigger ship than was originally proposed. Instead of adding length and height to an existing design, we proposed to rethink the entire layout and increase the maximum number of guests from 1,800 to almost 2,300. At the same time, we decided to increase the volume of the ship even more, from the original 50,000 tons to 72,000 tons. By doing this, we would increase the number of guests by 28 percent but the space available for guests by 44 percent, creating more room for more choices and a more enjoyable experience on board

Historically, people thought larger ships meant mass market and lower quality. We knew that we would need to do something substantively different to overcome this deep-rooted perception. The strategy we developed was to take half of the financial benefits of a larger ship's economies of scale and reinvest those savings to raise the quality of the ship.

Our larger ship would have better fixtures, better furnishings, and higher-quality materials than our guests expected. The new vessel would not just be large, it would make a statement about what a cruise ship could be. We could not be tentative. We needed to approach the design with purpose, not incrementalism.

No one was going to miss this change.

A new ship that offered more of everything would obviously be more expensive, but we were convinced that the market would pay for higher quality and more variety. We stole a line from advertising executive Jay Chiat and insisted that "good enough" isn't good enough.

This would prove to be one of the more controversial elements of our approach. Cargo shipping is a commodity business. Someone shipping a load of iron ore doesn't care how nice the ship is; they only care about the cost per ton of ore.

As a result, shipowners have a well-earned reputation for frugality. The idea that we would spend a lot of money to make a ship more attractive is not a comfortable concept for most shipowners. Rod McLeod, head of marketing and a true pioneer in the cruise industry, was a vocal advocate. "The increase in cost may be large in Norwegian Kroner," he argued, "but it will pay back in spades in US Dollars." Fortunately, his support carried a lot of weight.

We weren't chasing volume—we were building value.

Finally, we decided that if we were going to appeal to a broader market, we needed to reflect that in our marketing and in our product. Previously, the company avoided showing children or people with disabilities in advertisements, but now we identified families with children and the disabled community as two important markets. We needed to advertise to them, letting them know about the amenities we included to attract them like children's playrooms and better shipwide accessibility.

We weren't chasing volume—we were building value.

MORE THAN A YES

The date for the board meeting when we would finally present our findings approached quickly. This wouldn't be just any meeting; it was a defining one. It would focus on who we were and who we wanted to be. If we were right about the vision, the numbers would be great. If our view on the strategy was wrong, no amount of financial analysis could salvage it. Vision comes first and next comes alignment.

I had been experiencing a rollercoaster of emotions. When I was first asked to chair the committee, I was surprised and flattered. I viewed it as a great opportunity and was eager to show that I could do it well. But soon, that pride gave way to nerves—I was worried that these more experienced executives would see me as not having sufficient knowledge or experience to lead such a discussion.

As we became immersed in the project, those fears faded. I became energized, almost exhilarated. I didn't fall on my face. I was treated as a constructive voice, not an interloper. The committee worked well together and there was a tangible sense that we were defining something special—something that could elevate the company to a new level.

> **Vision comes first and next comes alignment.**

But as the board meeting date approached, I reverted to being nervous—afraid that I wouldn't be able to present our conclusions clearly enough or persuasively enough. Just last week, I was feeling confident; but today I could barely keep my hands from shaking.

The board meeting was held in Oslo, at the Norwegian Shipping Club, which celebrated the storied history of Norway as a center for maritime commerce for untold generations (although they tactfully skipped the Viking parts). That glorious history was unmistakable the moment you stepped inside. The space was decorated with so many ship models and nautical antiques that the scent of wood and leather was overwhelming. And its position above the Oslo Fjord gave the place a solemn, almost sacred feeling. One couldn't help but feel slightly awed—and a bit intimidated.

I hoped that this atmosphere would remind the board members that Norwegian shipping had thrived by being bold. Of course, part of me worried that the atmosphere might cause the opposite reaction, reminding them instead of the industry's adherence to tradition.

The tension in the room was palpable, the stakes high. There was particular concern about the size of the ship. No one had ever built a cruise ship of this scale, and some observers were complaining that ships half this size were already too big. This was a huge investment for the company. If we were wrong about the market's appetite for greater choice, it wouldn't just be disappointing; it could devastate the company.

In advance of the meeting, I talked at length with each of the owners and began to feel optimistic. However, I also knew that the dynamics of a meeting like this were unpredictable; it was not unusual for one negative voice to change the mood of such a discussion. At the meeting, we followed our principle of focusing on the strategy and dealing with the financials as support rather than as the centerpiece. I was heartened that the owners remained true to this process and focused on the strategic vision rather than the financial projections.

Still, the discussion spanned a wide range of topics—each with the potential to derail the project. "How can we be sure that our customers will like this new ship?" one person asked. "Are there enough itineraries for this new ship?" asked another. And a key question, "Can we find enough crew?"

As we discussed all these issues, I became increasingly confident that the conversation was going in a positive direction. The questions seemed aimed at ensuring that all aspects had been considered, not finding excuses for rejection.

When the vote was finally called, it was a unanimous decision to accept the steering committee's recommendations for an innovative new ship that would be dramatically larger and offer an unprecedented variety of activities. I was particularly heartened with the clear alignment between the vision of Ed and his team and the board.

It wasn't just a yes vote; it was enthusiastic support of a new vision for the business.

ANOTHER SURPRISE

Then came a surprise. I understood that the committee's purview was to make recommendations on long-term strategy. We had done that job, and I expected that was the end of our mission. Instead, almost as an afterthought, the other board members said that they assumed that the steering committee would continue to operate and to oversee the new ship's design and construction. Interestingly, it wasn't even discussed. It was simply commented on as a *by the way*.

While I was slightly miffed at being taken for granted in this way, I was also intrigued. Our strategic discussions had often veered into the practicalities of how to implement such changes, and I looked forward to participating in the design phase of the project. I relished the complexity of the problem. If you have unlimited funds, it's relatively simple to be the best at something; you just spend whatever it takes. Or, if the goal is to offer the least expensive product, you just spend as little as necessary to match whatever the competition is doing. Royal Caribbean was setting out to do a third thing: providing a top-quality vacation at a price our guests could afford. This called for balancing quality against cost and convincing the market that our product was something different. Achieving that goal would require a special kind of culture.

Our steering committee was beginning to develop that special culture before we realized it. We were now a team with passion and shared goals. We had managed to develop a clear alignment on an exciting path forward. But now, tangible decisions would have to be made about the more subjective design elements of a new ship.

Would our culture allow us to be bold and intentional? Or would we retreat to a safe place where incrementalism prevailed, and the final, underwhelming design seemed "fine" to everyone? What would guide us in the right direction? We were about to find out.

KEY TAKEAWAYS

- Long-term success often requires short-term sacrifices.
- Exceptional outcomes require messy, inefficient, and time-consuming collaboration, but a North Star—your ultimate goal—is essential to guide the way.
- True success demands unwavering focus on the long-term objective and purposeful action toward it; compromise and incrementalism won't cut it.
- Leading a company to greatness requires vision, but equally important is getting alignment on that vision from your team.

Take a different tack:

On sailing ships, a tack was originally a spike that was used to tack the sail to the mast. In the 1700s, the term evolved to describe shifting the sails to go in a new direction. Today, *changing tack* means to revise one's approach or course of action.

2

"Good Enough" Isn't Good Enough

We had set our goal as transformational change, but cruising wasn't known for transformational actions.

For many years, cruising had a certain formula. A guest's daily schedule was regimented, with set mealtimes and activities. You had formal nights with men wearing suits or tuxedos to dinner. You had your show after dinner, then the option of the midnight buffet. The company would focus maniacally on small, incremental improvements—changing an entrée on the dinner menu was a big deal—but fundamental shifts in product were rare.

Historically, our competition was viewed as being other cruise lines. Our company was fixated on performing as well as Carnival Cruises, which had introduced a very successful marketing and sales campaign. And we understood they were equally fixated on us.

However, the steering committee's foundational conclusion was that the cruise industry should not consider itself a specialized market competing among themselves. Rather, we should see ourselves as a small part of the larger and rapidly expanding vacation market. The real question wasn't how to surpass our rival cruise lines; the relevant question was how to inspire guests to choose our vacations over Marriott hotels, Walt Disney World, or Las Vegas resorts. This concept had been given lip service for years, but we saw an opportunity to make it a part of our core decision-making rather than a trite phrase that people recited without real conviction.

We had the goal, but how could we achieve it? How would we avoid making the kind of safe, incremental improvements that group decision-making is known for? If we only made incremental improvements with the new ship, we would plod along a path of mediocrity until we lost our distinctive approach.

We had to seize the opportunity to become something no one had seen before. We had to be transformational, and we needed to be intentional about it.

FROM APPROVAL TO ALIGNMENT

So far, we had no specific answers to that question, but already we felt we had two key elements for success: We had alignment. The board, the steering committee, and management now all shared a common vision. Too often, I've seen management get "approval" for a project without a real meeting of the minds.

But we didn't want just acceptance; we needed everyone on board (pun intended) with an aggressive and ambitious vision. We also had intentionality. Our new ship was intended to be a major step forward in design that no

> You don't want just acceptance; you need everyone on board with an aggressive and ambitious vision.

one could mistake for anything less. That goal was our North Star, and every action we took was oriented to achieving that bold intention. We had to make sure that every decision kept us pointed toward that overarching vision.

DESIGNING WITH PURPOSE

The steering committee now shifted its focus from general strategy to the specifics of innovating a ship that would carry us into the future. Fortunately, Ed Stephan had founded the company in 1968 based on his vision of designing ships specifically for the Caribbean. From the start, he had imagined new features never seen before, from smaller but more efficient cabins to bigger public rooms to an outsized pool deck with sun walk and, finally, to the iconic observation lounge called the Viking Crown. After working in the hotel industry and then another cruise line, Ed had started Royal Caribbean when he flew to Oslo and convinced three traditional Norwegian cargo-ship owners to support his revolutionary ideas for a cruise ship designed to sail in warm weather. He made innovation truly a part of Royal Caribbean's culture from the outset.

The Viking Crown Lounge on Royal Caribbean's first ship, *Song of Norway*.

Another advantage was the culture we had already started to establish in the steering committee. We had learned to engage in passionate but open disagreement about specific choices. Even during disagreements, the spirit in the committee was not *Whose idea will win?* It was *How can we do better?* One committee member would offer a suggestion or ask a question, which triggered a new thought in someone else, eventually leading to possibilities for improving ship design that none of us had imagined.

I recall an early committee meeting where the architect unveiled a rendering of a proposed room. The visual was stunning, but it was his passionate narrative that truly captivated us. He spoke with such emotion, saying the chairs were so comfortable you could easily fall asleep in them; the layout was fluid and gracious; the colors were vibrant. And then, with a hand over his heart and a sigh, he described the art pieces as simply exquisite. Confronted with this artistic rendering and his poetic storytelling, it was hard not to feel a sense of awe and think, *WOW, how quickly can we say yes?*

But then our head of food and beverage noticed a railing that was just barely visible in the rendering and asked, "Why is that railing there?"

The architect answered, "Because whenever you have a ramp, you must have a railing." He didn't mean to sound condescending, but he did. At that point, we realized that he wasn't inviting collaboration, he was defending his work.

And just that fast, the spell was broken. It quickly became clear that the head of F&B wasn't alone—none of us had realized that the design included a raised section with a ramp. And none of us liked the idea when we understood it.

It was like the moment when you're looking at a great painting and you don't know what to say, and then a helpful expert talks about a technical aspect, like the way the painter applied the brush strokes. A new world opens, and you can think and talk about how the painting came to be and how it makes you feel what you feel. Similarly, by concentrating on the details of a design and not being captivated by beautiful renderings, we began to look at the plans in a more thoughtful way.

ASKING QUESTIONS

In the steering committee meetings, we started asking questions and learning to talk about the cruise ship equivalent of brush strokes. We started to ask what we would never have thought to ask before: Does the raised section have to be there? What if we moved it and opened up that room in a different way? What would that be like for the guests who walked into the room? It wasn't individual genius, but it was the group process that made the difference.

We all benefited from what we came to call *cross-fertilization*. The committee was made up of people from many different specialties—from technical, operations, marketing, housekeeping, whatever. Each person had their own expertise, but we had learned during the early phase of the project that everyone should have a voice.

In past ship designs, the roles were rigidly siloed: the food and beverage director had the final word on anything culinary, the head of marketing controlled all consumer-facing decisions, and so on. No longer. Now, we had all gotten accustomed to opining on any topic and even questioning the subject-matter experts. The marketing guy now felt empowered to question assertions by the naval architect; the naval architect, in turn, felt free to challenge the navigator. Expertise was still respected, but now it was no longer sacrosanct.

Admittedly, sometimes it went too far. There were occasions where one person challenged another in their area of expertise, and they were so off base you just wanted to cringe. But the overall give and take was so overwhelmingly positive that we learned to live with the exceptions.

I loved playing devil's advocate in these meetings. Designing a cruise ship is amazingly complicated. There are so many aspects that have to be considered—from traffic flow to trash flow, from furniture design to fire safety, from crew functionality to guest comfort. I learned so much by participating in these discussions. I often find that the best way to get to a good answer is to argue it out.

We found that when designers had to explain something, they always learned from the process, and their designs got better. The very act of articulating their choices forced deeper thinking, exposed gaps, and sparked new ideas. The best way to understand something is to have to explain it to others.

We also found that since no one was confined to their area of responsibility, the junior participants felt freer to raise issues too. When everyone "behaves" (i.e., only speaks when they know enough to be confident of their question or comment), the more junior participants tend to stay silent. But here, everyone was commenting on areas outside their expertise, and this opening up was contagious.

For this new and ambitious undertaking, I looked for guidance wherever I could find it. One particular experience helped convince me about the importance of intentionality—of defining your North Star and sticking to it. My office at Gotaas-Larsen was on Victoria Street in London, and every morning, I took the train from our home in Wimbledon to Victoria Station. It was a very civilized way to commute (the British trains were a delight).

Between the train station and my office was the Apollo Victoria Theatre, which was built in 1930 and had hosted such great, traditional shows as *The Sound of Music* and *Fiddler on the Roof*. During the time we were designing our dramatic new ship, Andrew Lloyd Weber was opening his dramatic new show, *Starlight Express*. The show was unlike any traditional show and required massive changes to the structure of the building to accommodate his vision. Racetracks needed to be installed through the audience, the set had to be completely reimagined to accommodate roller-skating performers, and other technical innovations were required.

> **The best way to understand something is to have to explain it to others.**

It seemed like a massive undertaking just for one show, which might not even be successful. But every day for months, I saw huge construction crews transforming this grand Art Deco building into something no one ever imagined. And, when the show opened, it was an instant success, even to the nay-sayers. The crowds loved it, the critics loved it, and it was sold out for months. Ultimately, his production ran successfully for an impressive 18 years. (I can't resist pointing out that the ship we were creating had a successful run of 32 years.)

Weber's pushing through the inevitable objections to rebuild his theater was also a reminder that alignment is not synonymous with *consensus*. Alignment requires the participants to rally behind a single vision or plan, even when that vision is not everyone's first choice. Consensus, on the other hand, often involves compromises to satisfy outlying views. But this often leads to the least objectionable outcome rather than the best possible outcome. Consensus is much easier to achieve than alignment, and it feels good in the beginning because everyone is satisfied. Pleasing all voices feels good. But that good feeling only lasts a brief moment; the wishy-washy compromises endure forever.

Unfortunately, many people are uncomfortable with change, and to accomplish transformational change, you really need to accept that some people will not agree. The trick is to have enough dialogue that everyone contributes to the decision while not allowing a few voices to hold you back. Clarity and decisive leadership are essential to avoid settling for easy but mediocre outcomes.

Clarity and decisive leadership are essential to avoid settling for easy but mediocre outcomes.

CHALLENGING THE STATUS QUO

Today, large ships are an established feature of the industry, and different cruise lines compete to say they have the biggest. In the 1980s, however, many people assumed that a big ship meant a crowded ship, hard to get around, and lower in quality. It took many years and concentrated effort to prove that didn't have to be the case.

Based on our new, expansive view of the opportunity for Royal Caribbean, we decided to start the design work with a fresh sheet of paper. The naval architect responsible for new ship construction at Royal Caribbean was a man named Odd Martin Hallen. *Odd* in Norwegian doesn't mean strange; it comes from the Norwegian word for the sharp edge of a blade, and it was a very appropriate name for Hallen. Martin was as sharp as they come, and he never objected that we were essentially throwing away a year's worth of his efforts on the previous design.

During our vociferous debates about one design feature or another, Hallen would listen quietly. At the end, he would say, "Let me work on it." Then he would come back at our next meeting and take a different tack. Instead of focusing on one approach or the other, he would propose a solution that none of us expected but that usually met everyone's wishes.

We didn't have CAD (computer-aided design) back then, so we relied on what I've come to look back on as SAD (scissor-aided design). We cut and pasted and pinned paper sketches all over the walls. Ed Stephan added a separate area to his office for the drawings, and I dedicated my dining room at home to looking at the plans. My wife, Colleen, only laughed about my redecorating, which was fortunate for me. My kids, who were all under 10, may have found it funny that Daddy was hanging his drawings in the dining room at home, but the drawings were blueprints, so there wasn't much to hold their interest.

ARGUING THE PACE OF CHANGE

Not every steering committee discussion went smoothly.

Royal Caribbean had always been a data-driven organization, obsessively surveying guests about their experience. As soon as a ship returned to port after a cruise, the comment cards were the first item landed. They were quickly tabulated and the information disseminated to the individuals responsible for each area.

The company's culture was highly focused on these reports, and the management was obsessive about responding to any concerns or suggestions. It was an early application of the principle of continuous improvement and was an important factor in the company's success.

Now ironically, that same data was used by some to argue against truly transformational change. While all the members of the committee accepted that change was required, a vocal faction argued that more modest changes would be enough. They pointed out that our guests already loved our cruises. As one of the marketing executives observed, "Our guests already rate our cruises about the same as they rate chocolate. Why change something that is working so well?"

INTENTIONAL INNOVATION

One memorable debate centered on the Champagne Bar. We had never offered such a space. No guest had ever asked for one. We did sell a lot of champagne on our existing ships, but this fact cut both ways. One camp believed this proved that a dedicated space would be a valuable addition, while the other camp argued it proved the exact opposite—that we were already satisfying the demand, and we didn't need a new space.

At its core, this wasn't about champagne. It was about leadership—whether we would shape guest expectations or simply respond to them. Would we build something truly new, or make safe, incremental improvements?

The truth was that we were making an inference about what our customers didn't yet know they wanted, following the famous quote often attributed to Henry Ford: "If I had asked my customers what they wanted, they would have said a faster horse."

In the end, the decision required leadership and clarity. While all voices were heard, it was important to make a decision that was clear and understood by all. In this case, Ed and I decided to proceed with a dedicated champagne bar designed to rival the finest examples on land.

That result turned out to be one of the more striking features of our new ship and elevated the perception of the entire cruise experience. Whether you indulged in the Champagne Bar personally or just enjoyed it vicariously, it epitomized exactly the kind of elevated functionality we were building.

Admittedly, we didn't have a full consensus, but we did have alignment once the decision was made. The dissenters didn't love the decision, but once it was made, they supported it, and that is the definition of intentional leadership. Not blind obedience, but informed acceptance.

The Champagne Bar became a guest favorite—not just among champagne lovers but across the board. It offered something special and elevated the entire cruise. In fact, it was such a success that we included champagne bars on all subsequent ships until 2019, when tastes began to shift.

What started as a simple debate about champagne became so much more: a reminder that real innovation requires constant focus on your ultimate goal and the clarity that helps achieve alignment.

MAIDEN VOYAGE

By this point, I was far from the silent participant of my early days on the board. I had a lot to say. One day, Ed Stephan got frustrated and said, "Richard! You comment on this, that, and the other thing, but you've never even taken a cruise. You have no idea what you're talking about."

When I got home that night, I said to Colleen, "We can't let him keep saying that—especially since he's totally right! We have to take a cruise."

Both Colleen and I had always been in the camp of those who believe, "Cruising is great—just not for people like us." I had a high-pressure job at Gotaas-Larsen, and I liked vacations that took my mind off my work with activities that demanded my full attention. I loved scuba diving, because you have to focus 100 percent on breathing and maintaining neutral buoyancy. I also loved skiing, where you're desperately trying not to kill yourself as you fly down the mountain. I always preferred an active vacation, and I imagined that activity on a cruise meant shuffleboard and tying your tie for dinner. Also, I liked to vacation with my kids, and in those days, cruises were not for kids.

In my head, I understood that cruising appealed to all types. But in my heart, I felt I wasn't the type.

Colleen and I booked the shortest cruise we could find and asked to be assigned to a random table for six. We felt we'd learn more if the guests we met didn't know that I had a role at the company. We wrestled with the question of what to say when we sat down for dinner and our tablemates inevitably asked about our work.

Colleen, ever the positive one, said, "Maybe nobody will ask."

We agreed to keep my job a secret unless pressed. Then, fortune smiled on us. As soon as we sat down that first night at dinner, one of our tablemates said, "We're here to have a vacation, and we don't want to talk about work! We're not going to tell you what we do, and we don't want to hear about what you do. Let's just have a good time."

Colleen and I looked at each other and smiled. We couldn't believe our luck. Of course, the other couples couldn't uphold the agreement. We quickly learned that one was a computer programmer, one a salesperson, one had a shop repairing appliances, and one was a stay-at-home dad. Nevertheless, Colleen and I remained true to the agreement and stayed tight-lipped.

A little later in the meal, the waiter came over with a bottle of wine and said, "This is from the captain."

The others at our table looked surprised.

Then he brought another bottle and said, "This is from the hotel director."

Finally, he came back with a dozen business cards and said, "All these people would like to buy you a drink."

The people at the table obviously realized we were not just a random couple, but Colleen and I remained mum. We went to bed laughing—at ourselves and at the situation.

The next morning, our cabin steward greeted us with a joyousness that was contagious. He didn't seem to have a care in the world, and we realized that we didn't either. Normally, our day was filled with decisions and pressure about work and family. Here, we were free and easy.

We wandered ashore and had a fun time exploring an island we knew almost nothing about. It wasn't so much that we were learning about a new and interesting place but that we were learning about a new and interesting place *without having to make an effort.* Then came another refreshing dinner where we didn't have to impress anyone, just have a good time. And then the entertainment, an uplifting song and dance show with beautiful voices, captivating choreography, and energetic dancers.

Sleep and repeat.

We learned so much on that, our maiden voyage. We discovered how wrong our preconceptions were. This cruise was absolutely for people like us. I was amazed at how much we enjoyed that cruise and how right it was "even" for us.

We took that cruise because Ed had shamed me into it. But I came back changed—not just convinced about the product, but emotionally connected to it. Now I understood how important it was that we find ways to inform people like me: people who didn't understand how great a cruise vacation could be. Our job—now our mission—was to help create something special that would open people's eyes to the kind of joy they didn't yet know was waiting for them.

RECONCILING CONFLICTING GOALS

One key challenge in designing a bigger ship was to make it simple to get around. That might sound like an unsurprising goal, but cruise ship design starts not from the guest experience but from technical requirements that matter to engineers: where to place the engine room, how to dispose of trash, where large spaces like galleys go, and how to meet the extensive fire regulations.

These technical requirements are important; when you're out at sea, you can't call the fire department or borrow Grey Poupon from a neighbor. But while these requirements are important, the result is often ships that are confusing and tiring for visitors to walk around. This issue gets more significant as ships get bigger.

For smaller ships, with one dining room and relatively few public spaces, getting around is not such a problem. But our vision for this new kind of ship included greatly expanding guests' choices with unprecedented amenities: five restaurants, nine bars and lounges, an indoor café, a library with 2,000 books, a two-level Las Vegas–style showroom with a 15-piece orchestra and seats for over 1,000, plus a video game room, a children's playroom, a large health center and gym, a cardroom, a large hair salon, glass elevators, sweeping staircases, and fountains in marble pools. Did I mention the Champagne Bar?

We knew that we wanted to provide more venues to give our guests more choice of activities. But more venues meant a more complicated ship, and that conflicted with our goal of making it easy to get around. We wanted—we needed—this ship to feel *more* comfortable, *more* accessible than existing ships.

Reconciling conflicting goals is one of the fundamental issues every businessperson faces. In this case, the need for greater choice and variety seemed at odds with the need for being easy to get around. There was no obvious solution, and our initial instinct was to make compromises, like maps or signage. Those prevent you from getting lost, but they are a lousy solution. It's like tightening your belt on slacks that are too big or using air freshener to cover up a bad odor: They address the symptom rather than the cause of the problem.

After much discussion, we decided that the ship needed a heart, a core, a place everyone would be familiar with, a place that would provide an instinctual orientation. We decided to give the ship a tall atrium (we called it the Centrum) with all other areas radiating out from that central point. The idea was that the atrium would be so distinctive and central that everyone would know how to get there without thinking. Once they were there, they could get to all the other venues. Without having to look down at a map or up to read a lot of signs, guests could get where they wanted smoothly and easily.

The engineers rebelled against the five-story atrium. They pointed out that the steel decking on a ship helps keep the ship together, which naval architects consider to be a good thing. A large hole—they kept calling our Centrum a "hole"—would take away all that rigidity and strength. They also hated that it was in the middle of the ship. Having no steel in the core of the ship where stress is greatest seemed to them like a bad idea.

Their suggestion for helping guests to get around: more signs!

Odd Martin to the rescue. He pointed out that the new computer modeling allowed naval architects to calculate the stresses to a tolerance never before imaginable. Just as new methods of calculation had made flying buttresses on cathedrals unnecessary in the Middle Ages, modern computers now made it possible to design more flexible nautical structures. The engineers went back to work and designed an alternate way to provide the structural strength around the opening by reinforcing the steel decking above, below, and to the side of the atrium. (I refused to call it a hole.) In effect, they created a box around the opening that provided full structural support independent of the atrium inside the box.

The next big question was whether our Centrum would be marvelous or just cavernous. Fear was a big driver, because we were doing something nobody had done before, and the danger was that it would become an expensive disaster. In Miami, a new hotel had just been built with a large atrium—very grand and covered in expensive, dark marble. While visually striking, it felt cavernous, cold, and unwelcoming. They had spent a fortune to build it, and it backfired badly.

This hotel haunted me. We had so much momentum on the committee now toward "bigger is better" that I was terrified we would repeat the hotel's mistake. We finally decided that the entire steering committee needed to hold a meeting in that yawning hotel lobby. I wanted them to stand inside a good concept gone terribly wrong.

Our architect for large sections of the ship, including the Centrum, was a Norwegian by the name of Njål Eide. Njål was gentlemanly, but he was also tenacious and had an amazing eye for three-dimensional space. He loved curves, which are very graceful, but curves are also more expensive to build. (At one point, I sent him a ruler with a note that said, "This is called a straight edge, and on occasion, it can produce nice shapes at lower cost.") But for our Centrum, Njål stuck to his beloved curves. He was confident that the space would feel purposeful, not just a big opening that was there to make an impression.

During our committee meeting in the unpleasant hotel atrium, Njål made extensive comparisons between the hotel's mistakes and his very different plans, assuring us that our atrium would have none of the feeling of that hotel.

However, even with his assurances, we were still nervous; actually, we were terrified. I proposed building a full-size mock-up of the atrium out of plywood, just to get a sense of whether it was the right size. But the quote for building a mock-up was a million French francs (about $150,000 before the switch to the euro), and the committee saw that as ridiculously expensive. Njål and Martin made a few tweaks to improve the atrium and then insisted they were confident about it, so we let the building go on.

Until now, all Royal Caribbean ships had been built in Finland. The Finns were considered the world's best cruise ship builders, but French shipbuilding was improving quickly, and when we contacted Chantiers de l'Atlantique, they were hungrier for the order. Their terms were better, and they promised an extra degree of sophistication and beauty—"the French touch." We were convinced and placed the order at Chantiers de l'Atlantique in St. Nazaire, France.

UNVEILING THE ATRIUM

During construction, I visited the shipyard frequently, but every time I went to see the progress on the atrium, it was filled with scaffolding. I couldn't see anything, and I jokingly suggested that the shipbuilders were hiding it, masking a disaster until it was finished and paid for. Finally, Alain Grill, the chairman of Chantiers de l'Atlantique, called me in London.

"We're taking the scaffolding down," he said. "Come next week!"

Four of us went to walk the ship—Alain Grill, Odd Martin Hallen, Jean Le Tutour (the project manager for the yard), and me. It was a cold day, and the cold in France's northern coast is damp and penetrating. The steel of the ship seemed to radiate the cold. Despite my heavy winter coat, it was doing unpleasant things to my bones.

We walked down the corridor and sped up as we got closer to the Centrum. Alain said that he had waited to visit the space until we could see it together. I knew Jean had already seen it; he remained tight-lipped, but I took comfort from the smile he couldn't hide.

As we approached, I could see that it was still just raw steel, albeit fully shaped raw steel. The structure of the space was in place, and we were finally about to get a sense of what we had created.

We stood at the bottom on a raised platform, and we looked up. For a moment, we were frozen—not with the cold but with wonder. Finally, we could see the Centrum and it was . . . magnificent, simply breathtaking. The opening was unlike anything we had seen before on a ship. It just felt right! Five stories tall, with graceful staircases on each side, it was so big and impressive. But it was also human scale and felt very comfortable.

I looked over at Alain, and we smiled. Suddenly, Jean and I started dancing, right there on the platform. I don't know who started it, but there we were, one very dapper Frenchman and one rough American, dancing spontaneously. The atrium was just that beautiful. It was spectacular.

The Centrum was so admired that when Njål passed away in 2016, the first sentence of his obituary read "Architect Njål Eide, who brought soaring atria, sensational curves and dramatic dining rooms to cruise ships, died at age 85."

And today, no one builds a cruise ship without an atrium.

The finished Centrum with someone other than Jean and me dancing.

EN CHARETTE

Njål Eide loved anything curved, and he loved the color teal. He had an amazing eye for design, and his ability to envision three-dimensional spaces was exceptional. Every meeting with him was inspiring. However, there was an inevitable consistency of his designs. I felt that if we were going to offer guests as much choice as possible, we needed more variety in how the rooms looked. And that would require involving new architects (and a bit less teal).

It was one of the more raucous arguments at the committee. Ships are subject to much more stringent safety and technical requirements than land-based buildings, and there was a strong bias toward working with architects who understood the rules and had experience working in that environment.

I was still the neophyte in the room, and I tried to avoid unnecessary battles with other committee members. When the naval architects and the technical team in Miami rebelled against bringing in architects without specific training in cruise ship design, I scaled back my plan to a small experiment.

Could the committee agree to let one or two new architects work on a couple of less significant rooms? If they made technical errors, their mistakes could be fixed later. No one wanted to argue about two rooms, so in the absence of sustained objection, I asked my assistant to go to the library in London and find some promising architects.

She said, "I don't know anything about architects."

I said, "Well, I don't either. Go see who's won some awards."

She reluctantly did as I asked and returned with a list of 10 firms.

I then asked her to select three from the list for us to interview.

Again, she resisted, and again, I insisted.

Eventually (and with some muttering) she chose three firms, and we asked them to present design proposals to the committee for two rooms on board. When we saw the new ideas these firms presented, we were blown away. Beyond all our expectations, the new architects suggested innovative new ideas for layout and décor. Adding new blood invigorated the process.

Since then, we have followed a practice of bringing on at least one new firm of architects into every new class of ships. The challenge of teaching them the special constraints of shipbuilding remains, but the value of the new thinking justifies the effort.

We also tried another approach to design that served us so well that we use it to this day. Architects, like everyone else, are competitive people. The norm is that they jealously guard their work so that other architects can't steal their ideas. The resulting common practice is for competing architects to present sequentially, one by one in front of the client while the other architects wait outside.

But that has not always been the case. In the 1800s, there was a famous French Beaux-Arts school where the architecture students would work at home frantically up to the last minute to meet the deadline for submitting their designs. They were then picked up in a *charrette* (French for "cart") and taken to school with their designs. Often, the students would continue tweaking their designs in the cart, discussing the designs among themselves. This practice gave rise to the expression *en charrette*, meaning improving by working together. Today, a charrette is a working group discussing and refining designs collaboratively under tight deadlines.

Usually, a charrette involves the architect and other parties interested in the project. We decided that our steering committee had taken on many of the characteristics of a charrette and that we would invite all the architects to participate in our pseudocharrette. Even though they were technically competitors, we envisioned that their collaboration would lead to better designs.

I vividly remember one incident that more than validated our hopes: An architect presented her design for what we knew was a difficult space. The design was nothing short of brilliant—fresh, imaginative, and completely unexpected. She had somehow captured not just what we needed but something we hadn't even known to ask for.

When she finished, the room fell into a stunned silence. No one moved. No one spoke.

And then, without a word being said, we all broke into spontaneous applause. Nothing like that had ever happened before. It was an instinctive recognition of true excellence. It was a WOW moment.

> There is no motivator on Earth that matches self-motivation.

We took a break, came back, and the next architect got up to present his concept for a different room. He started by saying, "I'm about to present my proposal, but I don't think it's far enough along that you will applaud. However, when I come back next time, my presentation, too, will get applause!"

What was so valuable for me was to see that the architects were competing to show their best, not competing to beat each other. They each had their separate assignments, but sharing the presentations engaged their pride and pushed them to new heights. There is no motivator on Earth that matches self-motivation.

ANNIVERSARY DINNER

In 1986, Colleen and I hosted a Royal Caribbean board dinner at our house in Wimbledon. It happened to be our wedding anniversary, and Colleen and I had a tradition that we always ate pizza on our anniversary, tracing back to our first and second anniversaries when time and money were short. (Over the years, this tradition has saved me a lot of money on fancy dinners.)

This was our 17th anniversary, and it was unthinkable that we would ignore 16 years of tradition. But for the Royal Caribbean board, we also couldn't just order from the local pizza takeout as we usually did. Alf Clausen suggested that instead of having pizza as the entrée, we have it as the appetizer. Our guests loved it, and our tradition, which today remains unbroken for 56 years, was respected.

It was also a good meal with a real sense of optimism about Royal Caribbean's future.

After dinner, Arne Wilhelmsen and Cato Holmsen, the managing director of Skaugen, took me aside, saying, "We need to talk." That is always a scary opening line and usually bodes nothing positive.

They followed that with a blunt "You have been so vocal about our strategy that it is time for you to put up or shut up." Again, not a statement that instills positive thoughts.

Then came a real surprise: They asked me to leave Gotaas-Larsen and join Royal Caribbean in Miami as chairman and CEO.

It was a beautiful evening, and I was feeling no pain. I was incredibly flattered. I was 37 years old and Royal Caribbean was this incredible company, filled with amazing people. The opportunity was tremendous.

But ultimately, I had to say no, for two reasons that I felt were compelling.

The first reason was concern about the way Royal Caribbean was organized. I told Arne and Cato that I feared that Royal Caribbean's corporate structure was not going to allow the company to succeed in the long run. All decisions still needed to be unanimous, and the board, made up of people living in Norway and England, too often imposed our own views on a business that was run by Americans in America primarily for the American market.

One recent incident that had highlighted the issue for me was when the Miami management team proposed a tiny tweak to our iconic crown-and-anchor logo. The change was so subtle it would have been imperceptible to a normal human, but the board still debated it—at length.

I didn't have a view on the logo, but I didn't think it was right for us as a board to involve ourselves in such management decisions. My concern wasn't about branding; it was about proper governance. It was about the proper role of a board and how decisions got made.

To me, this incident and other similar ones indicated that our organizational structure was off kilter. At 21 years of age, Royal Caribbean was old enough to buy liquor; it was time to reassess the outdated legal and organizational structure.

My second reservation was personal. Colleen and I had built a life in the UK we cherished. England had become more than a temporary post; it was home. Our children were thriving in their British schools, we were immersed in a rich and inspiring cultural world, and we had formed enduring friendships.

Professionally, things had turned around. Gotaas-Larsen had weathered its storm and was on a strong, upward trajectory. We had arranged financing, found profitable charters for our ships, and were finally beginning to regrow the business. After years of struggle, it was incredibly rewarding to see Gotaas-Larsen finally thriving, and I couldn't wait to enjoy the success we had worked so hard to achieve.

With some reluctance, I told Arne and Cato that Colleen and I had made our decision: We didn't want to go. Not from Gotaas-Larsen. And not from England.

THE GREAT STORM

In 1987, Carnival went public. This sent reverberations throughout the cruise industry and shook up Royal Caribbean. The two cruise lines had always been a little like Coke and Pepsi. We were obsessed about what was happening at Carnival, and people at Carnival were obsessed about what was happening with us. We often talked about Carnival at our board meetings, and I assume they discussed us at theirs.

We believed that Carnival was very good at controlling costs, but we thought that their revenue wasn't as good as ours. As a result, we assumed our profitability was similar. However, when Carnival went public in June 1987, they announced a profit of $97.7 million. We were shocked. Royal Caribbean was doing only a little better than breaking even. It was clear that Royal had some things to learn about improving our finances.

Toward the end of 1987, Arne Wilhelmsen and Cato Holmsen approached me again. They said that they would like me to reconsider becoming chairman and CEO, but with two significant changes: They agreed to restructure Royal Caribbean so that it would function more like a normal corporation. And they said that the job could be part time. I could continue to live and work in London at Gotaas-Larsen and commute as needed to Miami.

It did sound exciting. By then, Colleen had just given birth to our fourth child—Jessica, a gorgeous baby girl. Despite this, Colleen was supportive of the revised job offer, saying it was a unique opportunity that I should accept. In addition, both Ed Stephan and Alf Clausen supported it. So, I accepted, with thanks and eagerness. We agreed to make it effective at the end of the first quarter of 1988. I would become chairman and CEO of Royal Caribbean while continuing as joint managing director of Gotaas-Larsen.

But 1987 still had more surprises for us. October started on a good note: Gotaas-Larsen had survived the shipping industry collapse, and our shares had grown from a low of $2.00 to $38.00; I had just visited *Sovereign of the Seas* in St. Nazaire, and she looked amazing; I was approaching my 40th birthday; and I was about to join Royal Caribbean as chairman and CEO. Rarely have so many things come together so nicely.

But then on Friday, October 16, the Great Storm of 1987 hit England. This extratropical storm was the worst to hit the British Isles since 1703 (only the British would have records so far back). The storm killed 18 people and blew down 15 million trees (including a stately oak in my garden).

Then, three days later, dubbed Black Monday, the New York Stock Exchange dropped 23 percent, the largest single-day drop in American history. The Great Depression had been bigger and longer, but the Great Depression didn't begin with such a huge one-day swing. Suddenly, the prices of homes were in free fall. Pension plans were losing value.

Our competitor, Norwegian Cruise Line, was forced to cancel its initial public offering. The world was looking like a darker place.

The largest shareholder in Gotaas-Larsen was the financier George Soros, who called me on Thursday of that week. My previous discussions with George had been very warm. I liked him and appreciated his confidence in investing in Gotaas-Larsen when so many people thought he was crazy to do so. He was very supportive of us, and he appreciated how well our turnaround program at Gotaas-Larsen had performed.

But this call was definitely not warm.

George opened up without any of our usual preliminaries, "Richard, you need to cancel the order for the *Sovereign of the Seas*!"

I said, "George, we can't cancel the order. The ship's finished. It's almost built."

He said, "I know it's almost done, but you've got to cancel, because nobody's ever going to want to cruise again. Everybody just feels poor now, and if they feel poor, they won't buy a cruise. You should act before the shipyard realizes how bad the future will be."

I said, "George, even if that's true, the ship is built. We can't cancel. They're already vacuuming the carpets!"

He said, "You may have to pay them a penalty, but you've got to cancel."

Of course, I was eager for our new ship to be delivered, because I felt it would validate our perceptions of the market. Also, the cruise industry had proven resilient in previous recessions, so I didn't share the stock market's widespread pessimism. Neither argument seemed likely to change George's mind, so I reminded him that Gotaas-Larsen owned only one-third of Royal Caribbean. We couldn't unilaterally demand the cancellation of a contract.

He said, "Well, you've got to do *something*!"

Fortunately, despite the severity of Black Monday, the 1987 crash was short lived. Within six months, the stock market was back to where it had been.

THE LAUNCH OF THE MEGASHIP ERA

Finally, on January 15th, 1988, *Sovereign of the Seas* was officially named by her godmother, Mrs. Roslynn Carter. President and Mrs. Carter then joined 2,000 other guests as *Sovereign* made her maiden voyage from the Port of Miami.

Taittinger, the great champagne producer, offered to provide the champagne for the party and the traditional breaking of the bottle against the ship's bow. They offered us a Jeroboam for the naming, a large bottle that held three liters of champagne, but we felt that was too small for the occasion. Next, they offered a Methuselah, with 6 liters, and then a Balthazar, which holds 12, and finally a Nebuchadnezzar, 15 liters, the equivalent of 20 bottles of champagne.

We replied that those are all very big bottles, thank you, but this cruise ship is bigger than anybody's ever seen before; can't you do better? And so they custom made a 25-liter bottle, the largest bottle of champagne in the world, to celebrate the largest ship in the world. To this day, the 25-liter bottle is called a *Sovereign*.

A Sovereign for a *Sovereign of the Seas*.

The first guests on board, including more than 1,700 travel agents and 125 members of the news media, were dazzled. They talked about the beauty of the ship and the spectacular spaces on board, including the new Viking Crown Lounge, a 250-seat cocktail lounge wrapped around the ship's smokestacks 14 stories above the water. They raved about the Centrum. They lauded the higher-quality finishes and curated art. As a reviewer from the *Chicago Tribune* wrote, "The eyes flit from brass to shiny glass and posh decor in absolute amazement as the ship's staff welcomes you aboard. The ship is dotted with $1.7 million in art . . . and is amazingly quiet and vibration free."*

We had done it. *Sovereign* was profitable from her maiden voyage on, and her guest satisfaction scores were the highest in the company's history. *Sovereign*'s larger scale—once seen as a risk—became something to celebrate, a new kind of cruise luxury with a far broader appeal. They even coined a name for such ships: *megaships*. And *Sovereign of the Seas* was the first.

I didn't realize it at the time, but the concept of megaships was a turning point in Royal Caribbean's history and indeed the history of the industry. It offered new, creative opportunities for ship design. More importantly, it made the goal of becoming truly competitive in the vacation market closer to reality.

STEERING TOWARD THE FUTURE

It was against this background that I prepared to take up my new role as part-time chairman and CEO of this exciting company.

---

* "The Sovereign." *Chicago Tribune*, 17 Jan. 1988.

KEY TAKEAWAYS

- To achieve transformational results, one has to pursue transformational changes rather than relying on small, incremental improvements.
- Effective collaboration, though often messy, can lead to remarkable outcomes.
- Establishing a clear vision acts as a guiding North Star.

To show one's true colors:

To show one's true colors means to reveal one's real character or nature, especially when it differs from the initial impression. In the seventeenth century, colors referred to the flag or pennant that ships were required to fly at sea. Pirates would sometimes fly false flags to approach their targets without arousing suspicion. When they were close enough to attack, they would *show their true colors* by raising their actual pirate flag.

3

A 40-Day Countdown to an Uncertain Future

By May 1988, *Sovereign of the Seas* had been WOWing guests for four months. Guest satisfaction scores were at record levels and profits were up nicely. The future was looking bright, and we were turning our attention to building on the success of *Sovereign*.

Then, one morning, Jack Seabrook, the chairman of Gotaas-Larsen, called with shocking news. Carnival, the largest and most powerful cruise line in the world, wanted to buy Royal Caribbean. With that news, our future, our vision, everything we had been working toward was in play. I had only been Royal's CEO for a few weeks, and suddenly, this call sounded like it might change everything.

The following week, Jack and I flew to Rome and drove to Civitavecchia to meet Carnival's principal owners—its founder and chairman, Ted Arison, and its president and Ted's son, Micky Arison. The meeting was held on Ted's yacht, *Mylin II*, named for Ted's wife, Lin. We ate lunch and talked on the aft deck and enjoyed a beautiful Mediterranean afternoon.

Ted and Micky were gracious hosts, and the conversation was pleasant and nonconfrontational. We focused on two primary issues: the sale price and Carnival's insistence on gaining control by owning at least 51 percent of Royal Caribbean. Ted and Jack did most of the talking, while Micky and I responded to specific questions as they arose.

I was not uncomfortable in the meeting, but I had mixed feelings about its potentially monumental outcome. A sale of Royal Caribbean to Carnival would mean profits both for Gotaas-Larsen and for me as a shareholder. But as chairman and CEO of Royal Caribbean, I wanted to know if Carnival believed in the work done by the steering committee. Would they want the company to fulfill our vision of a bigger company offering an upgraded product in a bigger market? Or were they just looking to buy out a competitor and continue business as usual? Those questions didn't come up, and there was no opportunity to ask them.

By the end of the afternoon, it was clear that Carnival and Gotaas-Larsen were far apart on the issues. Jack and I thought a higher price was appropriate (who wouldn't?), and, in any case, convincing either the Skaugens or Wilhelmsens to sell their shares seemed highly unlikely. I assumed the negotiation was over, and I went home to juggle my two jobs.

Two months later, Jack called and said, "Guess what? We've finalized a deal. Carnival has agreed to buy our stake in Royal Caribbean, and the Skaugens have agreed to sell their stake at the same price." This was astounding news. While I wasn't shocked that Carnival would pay a good price—and the amount was surprisingly high—I never expected that either of the Norwegian owners would sell.

The Skaugens had one more surprise for us. While they were willing to do a deal that would undercut the Wilhelmsens, they weren't willing to do it without giving their partners a fair chance to come out ahead. They would only sell if Wilhelmsen had a right of first refusal.

This last point may sound innocuous, but it was huge.

The right of first refusal gave Wilhelmsen the right to match Carnival's offer and take over Royal Caribbean on the same terms that Carnival had offered. The only catch was that Wilhelmsen would have to exercise the right within 40 days. If Wilhelmsen could raise $300 million in cash (plus another $250 million in debt), they could buy the Gotaas-Larsen and Skaugen shares and become the sole owner of Royal Caribbean. However, if they couldn't raise that much money, then Carnival would buy the shares, and Royal Caribbean would become a subsidiary of Carnival. In that case, Wilhelmsen would own one-third of a cruise line completely controlled by Carnival.

The future of Royal Caribbean was at a critical juncture and would be decided in only 40 days. Carnival was offering a very high price based on Royal Caribbean's historical profitability but a very low price if our vision of the future was right. I believed in Royal Caribbean's potential to transform its results and help lead our entire industry based on our new growth and innovation strategy.

My personal hope was that Wilhelmsen would win. I had come to respect the Royal Caribbean team and wanted to see the company thrive independently rather than see it swallowed up by the larger Carnival organization. I was convinced that Royal Caribbean on its own was about to achieve exciting things. That would never happen within the confines of the Carnival organization, regardless of how good that organization was.

As part of their due diligence, Carnival asked for a tour of *Sovereign of the Seas* for their senior management. Once on board, they were gracious and complimentary, but they made it clear that they saw greater opportunity for Royal to build smaller ships designed to attract older and more affluent passengers, like Holland America (then the second most profitable cruise line). That was not the message I was hoping to hear!

From a strictly business point of view, Gotaas-Larsen and Skaugen got the same payout regardless of who the buyer was, but we each had our personal preferences. Emotionally, I was rooting for Arne Wilhelmsen to be the buyer while Jack Seabrook favored Carnival's deal. Interestingly, Morits Skaugen, whose agreement made the Carnival deal possible, was clearly hoping that his fellow Norwegian would win the day.

There wasn't much time. Forty days was an extremely short time for anyone to raise the capital and complete a transaction of this magnitude—let alone a modest-size Norwegian ship owner.

Maybe the only realistic offer was Carnival's.

A SURPLUS OF SUITORS

The shipping community is very close-knit, and gossip is its lifeblood. This transaction was one of the largest and most exciting deals in the Norwegian shipping industry, and the press gleefully reported every rumor. Almost every day, there were stories setting forth new reasons why Wilhelmsen would be unable to match Carnival's offer. Journalists pressured Arne to comment, and I think they were particularly sour toward him because he refused to give them a quote that would help them sell newspapers.

Arne steadfastly refused to say anything negative about Carnival. He refused to say anything negative about Gotaas-Larsen or Skaugen. He wouldn't reveal his plans. He simply said, "I'm exploring my alternatives." Staying quiet amid such a cacophony of comments by others demonstrated amazing willpower, and Arne did it beautifully.

But Arne wasn't quiet or inactive in private.

Privately, he made it clear that he had no intention of becoming just a minority shareholder in a company controlled by someone else. But he was also pragmatic and knew that, to take over the entire company, he needed a partner. He swiftly hired the investment bank

Lehman Brothers, which then dispatched a team to our offices in Miami, where we began educating them on the cruise industry.

By coincidence, Arne Wilhelmsen happened to be traveling through Charles de Gaulle Airport in Paris one day and ran into Paul Baquert, head of Banque Indosuez's shipping department.

Paul asked Arne, "How is your deal going? I know somebody who might be interested in being your partner. If I can make that happen, would you give me the same commission you're offering to Lehman?" Arne agreed. Now he had two big banks working on potential deals for him.

Paul called Sammy Ofer, an Israeli shipowner, who was very wealthy, very canny, and known for acting quickly and decisively. Sammy told Paul, "This deal sounds interesting, but it's not shipping. It floats, but that doesn't make it shipping; it's hospitality. However, we are friends and partners with Jay Pritzker, who owns Hyatt Hotels and obviously has hospitality expertise. Maybe, together with Jay, we can do a reasonable deal."

Within hours of Arne's chance encounter at the airport, Sammy and Jay were discussing the concept of partnering with Arne. A few hours later, Jay called me in Miami and said, "How soon can you come to Chicago and talk to us?"

Knowing that the 40-day countdown clock was running, I said, "There's a plane first thing in the morning, but if you'll give me a few more hours, I can bring a team of people and reams of information in the afternoon."

But Jay said, "No, just come. We'd like to focus on the big picture, and we can review the details later."

Early the next morning, I flew to Chicago and went straight to Jay's apartment, not to his office. We talked all day. That night, we went to a football game (the Bears lost), and the next morning, we reconvened and talked some more.

Sammy and his son Eyal flew in from Israel to join the conversation. They, along with Jay and his son Tom, kept asking me general and philosophical questions about the cruise industry: "What is your vision for the business? Where do you see the growth coming from? What are the biggest risks?"

We spent three intense days in wide-ranging dialogue about the cruise industry, its people, its opportunities, and its risks. I found it exhilarating to have some of the sharpest and most insightful minds in business so interested in Royal Caribbean's potential. After discussing the big picture vision, we moved on to a detailed review of the numbers. Taking the topics in this order made me feel good about their priorities. Too many people approach it the other way around.

At the same time, Lehman Brothers was preparing a separate plan of their own. We didn't know it at the time, but they were getting ready to launch a fund to invest in businesses directly. Instead of arranging for others to do deals, Lehman was looking to do deals for themselves. And it gradually became clear to us that they saw the cruise industry as a bold and prestigious way for them to make a name for themselves in the then-novel field of private equity. More than just helping Arne find a partner, Lehman now wanted to be that partner.

Suddenly, the deal to take over Royal Caribbean had three powerful suitors, and the cruise industry was on the threshold of a major shift. It was clear that this sector was transitioning from a niche market catering to a narrow audience to becoming a significant industrial player.

The surge of interest by such major players was thrilling and validating, but too much *thrilling* quickly morphs into *scary*. I enjoy a good game of poker, but when the stakes get this high, I get very nervous.

One issue that arose was that all three suitors—Carnival, Lehman, and Pritzker/Ofer—needed extensive assistance and information from Royal Caribbean to complete their analysis of the opportunity. In effect, they each wanted to duplicate the steering committee's analysis for themselves. But they wanted to do it in a few weeks instead of six months.

It was difficult satisfying any one of the three and impossible to satisfy them all. As the pressure mounted, it was the lawyers who panicked. Each party's lawyers threatened to sue, saying we weren't doing enough to support their client's proposal. Even the lawyers for my own company, Gotaas-Larsen, threatened to sue, afraid that the Wilhelmsen deal would fall through, and, in the chaos, Carnival would walk away. Under normal circumstances, I would hire my own lawyer and was reminded several times of the adage that "the person who represents himself has a fool for a client." But I knew that if I was represented by counsel, it would kill true communication, so—foolish or not—I didn't hire one.

To avoid any appearance of a conflict, I offered to resign from Royal Caribbean. When my resignation was refused, I offered to leave Gotaas-Larsen. That resignation, too, was refused, and the drama continued. I don't recall another time when I was so busy meeting with people and yet felt so alone. Every meeting, every conversation felt like a negotiation—I felt like I was constantly having to represent something or defend something. And I worried constantly whether I had the skill or experience that was needed.

Amid all the pressure there in Miami, Colleen visited from England with our four kids, including our one-year-old. The reunion was a welcome relief but reminded me how difficult it was to be so far from them the rest of the time. And as happy as I was to see them, I was upset that I couldn't spend the time with them that I needed (and that I owed them).

NEARING THE FINISH LINE

Arne kept his options open, but he was leaning toward the Pritzker/Ofer deal. He had faith in the industry and in Royal Caribbean's ability to grow and prosper. He knew the Lehman alternative would take Royal Caribbean off its growth trajectory and focus it on getting immediate cash to repay Lehman's debt. In effect, the Lehman deal offered lower financial risk but at the cost of hamstringing the company's future. Arne was steadfast in his determination to ensure Royal

Caribbean remained both independent and successful. His focus and resolve impacted us all and left a mark that endures.

What happened next was shocking. On about day 30 (of 40), Lehman Brothers asked for a private lunch to discuss the deal. I was confused; after endless hours of detailed reviews with our financial team, they now wanted a meeting alone with me?

Toward the end of the meal, I remember asking myself if they would ever get to the real reason for the meeting. So far, it had been a pleasant lunch at a nice steakhouse in downtown Miami, but nothing particularly notable.

While we were racing the clock to finalize a deal to keep Royal Caribbean independent, Lehman insisted on having an inconsequential bankers' lunch? Finally, they got to their point: They suspected that Arne might be leaning toward the Pritzker/Ofer alternative, and they knew that Arne respected my views. They told me that if Arne agreed to their deal, "it would be appropriate that you be given a carried interest of 10 percent of the company over five years."

I said that sounded suspiciously like a bribe. Lehman Brothers was showing their true colors.

"Of course not," they responded with apparent sincerity. "This is sweat equity. You would simply be paid for the success of the business."

I guess if you phrase it correctly, a bribe is not a bribe.

I was stunned. I wasn't sure if I should feel insulted or complimented. Should I react in a strong way or just go home? I felt unclean. I wanted to express my outrage in some dramatic fashion, but no gesture felt right. Instead, I finished my tea as politely as I could and walked out without saying anything further.

I never told Arne about the lunch, and I never spoke to Lehman again. But all these pressure tactics—the threats of lawsuits, the endless demands for information, the offer of special compensation—taught me something. The steering committee had been right about the potential for Royal Caribbean to succeed in an expanding cruise industry, and the proof was how desperately these major suitors were fighting for their deals.

The little Norwegian cruise company had come of age. The cruise industry was now high finance.

Arne made his decision in favor of Pritzker/Ofer, but we still had to close the deal.

Day 39 fell on November 4, and it seemed we would make the deadline with just 24 hours to spare. Everyone assembled in London at the headquarters of our lawyers Watson, Farley, & Williams. All the participants were represented—a total of about 30 people including the buyers, the sellers, the lenders, the lawyers (from eight different firms, argh), and finally the corporate secretaries. All the paperwork had been prepared and reviewed. The purchase price had been collected and organized in two banks so the transaction could close smoothly.

We were ready to rock and roll.

The documents were assembled in the middle of the table. It took about four hours to do a final check of the papers and satisfy all the participants that they were in order. Buttons were pressed, calls were placed, and the wheels of the transfer were officially set in motion.

And then 300 million dollars vanished.

The new partners had raised that money to complete the deal, but when they issued the instructions to pay, nothing was transferred—zilch, nada. Three hundred million dollars had just disappeared. We were told that the international banking system processed millions of transactions each day and that, "occasionally," one or two were "misplaced." We were also assured that these errors were "always" fixed. But we didn't care about anyone else's experience. We were worried about *our* money—the $300 million we needed to complete the transaction.

The bank assured us they were working hard to find our money. They were sure they would do so soon, but as every hour went by, the tension rose.

At 6:00 p.m., after hours of looking, the banks reported that they hadn't yet found our cash, but they were making "progress." At 9:00

p.m., they reminded us of how many transactions they processed every day. At 11:00 p.m., there was still no sign of our $300 million. Even worse, the bank now informed us that their computer shut down every night at midnight for a few hours of preventative maintenance.

If we missed the deadline—now only 24 hours away—Carnival would proceed with their deal. (We were even warned that they had a plane on the tarmac ready to take off if we were late.)

Every hour, we checked for updates, and every hour, the bank assured us that they were working hard on it.

We had nothing to do while we waited for the bankers to find our money except to contemplate the consequences of failure. We were so close. Our lawyer, Martin Watson, regaled us with stories of other tense closings, and I tried singing to lighten the mood. ("Oh, What a Beautiful Morning" is a perennial favorite.)

One member of our group was a French official who was a critical player in the transaction and who had already put more effort into our deal than we had any right to expect. In an effort to make her more comfortable, we booked a suite at the Savoy Hotel to use while we waited. She declined. As the length of the delays became clearer, we extended the offer of hotel rooms to everyone. As one, they said, "We're here. We're not leaving until this deal is done and every detail complete."

No one left the room that night. We stayed there until, finally, at 5:00 a.m., one of the bankers burst into the room saying, "They found it."

I don't remember much after that. With the entire team together in one place, the deal closed at 6:00 a.m. on the very last day allowed under the right of first refusal. I remember we felt good but mostly worn out. In retrospect, we let the moment slip by—no champagne, no dinner, no acknowledgment of what we'd accomplished. We didn't do any of that, and we should have.

Our closing day, November 5, is also Guy Fawkes Day in Britain. It commemorates the foiling of the 1605 Gunpowder Plot to blow up

Parliament. (Only the English, with their love of irony and history, would celebrate a near-disaster almost 400 years later.) That night, there were fireworks and bonfires across the country. I was completely oblivious to it all, both the holiday and the not-quite-as-historic development for Royal Caribbean.

Soon after, three changes significantly improved my life. First, two British brothers bought Gotaas-Larsen for a price of $48.00 per share. Our share price when Alf and I took over was $2.00 per share. Seeing such an increase in just seven years was exhilarating. Second, I switched from part-time chairman & CEO of Royal Caribbean to full-time, recognizing that it really was a full-time job. And last but not least, Colleen and I decided that commuting between London and Miami was not compatible with a reasonable home life with our four wonderful children. It was time for us to move to Miami, where we have been proud to live ever since.

KEY TAKEAWAYS

- Critical junctures define a company's future; moments of negotiation or decision-making can alter the entire course of a business.

- Managing conflict requires navigating competing interests, balancing different stakeholders—partners, investors, and personal values—in high-stakes deals.

- Pressure can reveal true character; how you handle intense stress and difficult choices often shapes your legacy.

- Reconciling conflicting goals can produce a result better than either would on their own.

Gross ton:

In the Middle Ages, wine was shipped in a cask that the French called a *tun*. Ships were measured by how many of these casks (or tuns) they could hold. A tun was therefore a measure of volume, not weight. *Tun* evolved to be written *ton* and, today, is referred to as a *gross ton* or GT.

Some comparative ship sizes: *Mayflower*, 180 GT; clipper ships, 1,000 GT; *Song of Norway* (Royal Caribbean's first ship), 18,000 GT; *Titanic*, 46,000 GT; *Sovereign of the Seas*, 73,000 GT; *Icon of the Seas*, 248,000 GT.

4

Grow or Die

Talk about pressure.

One week after the deal closed in London, I had a meeting in New York with my new bosses, the three new owners of Royal Caribbean. The goal was simple: alignment on a shared vision for the company.

Two years earlier, I had turned down the job as CEO because we didn't have that alignment. At the time, I feared there was a disconnect between the direction envisioned by different members of the board, the management, and the rest of the company. Too many decisions were compromises among people with different visions, and that approach doesn't work. Instead of clear direction, we often ended up with half measures. I didn't know which side was right, but I knew that splitting the baby was the wrong answer.

One early example was the marketing budget. One side wanted a major expansion, believing more marketing would drive more revenue. The other argued Royal Caribbean was already popular, and extra spending wasn't necessary. The compromise? A moderate increase—enough to be noticeable but not enough to move the needle. That kind of middle-ground thinking might have worked for Goldilocks and the Three Bears, but it's a bad way to run a business.

Then came a seismic shift. Royal Caribbean now had new owners—three titans of commerce: Arne Wilhelmsen, Jay Pritzker, and Sammy Ofer. They had just invested $550 million in Royal Caribbean—not in what it was but in a vision of what it could become. And they expected to hear me articulate exactly how we would make that vision a reality.

No pressure.

Hoping for an open, casual conversation, I suggested we avoid the formality of a conference room. Instead, we met in Jay's suite at the Grand Hyatt Hotel, perched above Grand Central Station, in Manhattan. This was a once-in-a-lifetime opportunity to align on the company's future. During the takeover process, we had explored opportunities at a high level. Now, it was time to make decisions. There were just four of us in the room, focused on defining the future we envisioned for the company and the steps we intended to take to get there. Our goal was clear: achieve alignment around a single, cohesive strategic vision for transformative growth.

ROYAL CARIBBEAN

1988 Strategic Plan

1. Don't screw it up
2. Improve revenue
3. Improve revenue
4. Control costs

During the meeting, I presented the core pillars of our proposed strategic plan. The presentation was brief—just one page—but it conveyed everything we needed to move forward.

These four points might appear to oversimplify the challenges of running a complex business. But the intent of these four points was not to impress with a long, exhaustive presentation. Rather, I hoped to focus on a few key points that would provoke a rigorous dialogue. The best alignment comes from working together through the bigger issues and arriving at a shared conclusion.

The first point, *Don't screw it up*, was not a general admonition to behave. It was a reminder that Royal Caribbean was already a successful operation with dedicated employees and a highly loyal following. While improvements were important, they had to be thoughtful. We needed to build on the company's strong foundation, not undermine it. Improve? Yes. Tear down and rebuild? No.

The second point, *Improve revenue*, represented our greatest opportunity. Royal Caribbean had a fantastic product, but we hadn't yet achieved sufficient scale or pricing that reflected the true value we offered our guests. This point underscored the need to enhance the profitability of our existing operation to support our long-term aspirations.

By repeating the second point again as the third point (no, it wasn't a typo), I hoped to use humor to emphasize its importance. Although it was the same wording as the second point, it pointed to an entirely different opportunity. While point two focused on the opportunity for our existing product, point three highlighted opportunities for future growth—such as newer, more advanced ships, improved operational excellence, and other enhancements.

The final point, *Control costs*, highlighted my concern that product enhancements can easily result in cost overruns. While offering new and improved services was essential, we had to be sure we did so at a reasonable cost. But I deliberately used the word *control* rather than *reduce* to emphasize that this was not a cost-cutting exercise but, rather, an exercise in prudence. The goal was to ensure we remained efficient and financially sustainable. We needed to do more for less, not less for less.

> **We needed to do more for less, not less for less.**

While our discussions during the takeover process gave me confidence that we would reach consensus on these four guiding principles, I was nervous. All three individuals were strong-willed and had become successful by making their own independent decisions. Would they unite behind a new business model for Royal Caribbean, or would we get bogged down in different approaches to the next steps?

I needn't have worried. Over a full day of discussions, we examined and reexamined and re-reexamined every aspect of the opportunity. We explored different strategies, tested various scenarios, and took turns playing devil's advocate to challenge our assumptions. Ultimately, it

Left to right: The author, Sammy Ofer, Arne Wilhelmsen, and Jay Pritzker.

felt like a Vulcan mind meld,* combining our individual perspectives into one. Despite our diverse backgrounds—different nationalities, industries, and even native languages—we reached a shared vision.

In the end, we were all energized by the opportunity to grow a thriving enterprise with the power of transformation and innovation. We could almost taste what the outcome would be. While this was just the beginning of our journey, we were ready and resolute in our commitment to see it through.

WHERE THE PUCK WOULD BE

At last, the operating management had a North Star to guide our path, and we had the strong support (indeed encouragement) of the board for hewing to that course. The challenge was to make sure we executed the mission with intentionality. We couldn't make half-hearted compromises. We had to execute every decision at every level with a conscious commitment to achieving our four strategic goals.

But where to start? In my opinion, the highest potential opportunity to increase our revenue was to build on the success of *Sovereign of the Seas*. Our first megaship had been a game changer. It proved the value of innovation in a tangible way—and it became far more profitable than we ever imagined. But despite its success, we remained a midsize player, neither large enough to lead the industry nor small enough to be a nimble disruptive startup.

Rather than waiting for clear proof of demand before placing an order for a new ship, the partners agreed to take an aggressive approach, targeting the much larger, untapped market that was ready

---

* It has been pointed out to me that not everyone knows what a Vulcan mind meld is. If true, it would be a sad commentary on the current state of cultural literacy. I can only suggest that any reader who does not immediately understand the reference should educate themselves by watching at least five Star Trek movies. I can recommend *Star Trek IV: The Voyage Home*.

to be claimed. As Wayne Gretzky famously put it, what made him better than other hockey players was that he didn't skate to where the puck was; he skated to where the puck would be. We committed to go where demand for cruises would be in the future, not where it had been in the past.

Was it risky to commit hundreds of millions of dollars to buying new ships before we had proof of sufficient demand for *Sovereign*? Yes. But failing to place the order was an even greater risk; it would leave us stuck in the perilous middle ground, where we risked being squeezed out of relevance.

The choice was to grow or to die.

The original steering committee had taken months of analysis to propose ordering one ship. Now in less than half an hour, we had agreed to order two more. Then, Sammy Ofer surprised us. Sammy looked at us through his signature black-framed glasses and said, "This new approach will mean ordering a new ship each year for the foreseeable future."

At first, we assumed he was exaggerating. With Sammy you could never quite tell, but we did know that Sammy never said anything without a real purpose behind it.

Within a month, we placed the orders with the French shipyard. We named our new ships *Monarch of the Seas* and *Majesty of the Seas*. Both had all the features that made *Sovereign* such a success, but they weren't pure sisterships.

Building a new ship involves large, fixed costs for design and engineering, and it is common to make subsequent ships that are essentially duplicates of the first. This significantly reduces the cost of subsequent ships, but it also severely limits any changes or improvements. And that constrains our options for continuous improvement based on lessons learned (and there are always lessons learned from building and then operating a new ship).

Some improvements are relatively minor. For example, guests on *Sovereign* commented that the downlights in the massage rooms glared in their eyes. As part of my due diligence, I personally tested the massage rooms and checked the lighting. After many massages diligently taken to study the issue, I concluded that the complaint was valid. We redesigned the ceilings and installed cove lighting. I booked additional massages to ensure the issue was properly resolved. (It was a sacrifice I was willing to make.)

Other improvements were more significant. For example, one of the new features on *Sovereign* was the Windjammer Café, an elegant and spacious buffet restaurant that was a highly novel feature at the time. The Windjammer was such an overwhelming success that we wanted to double its size on *Monarch* by expanding its footprint and adding a second level. But what seemed like a simple change came with a complex engineering challenge. Adding that much weight high on the ship changes the hydrodynamics of the vessel. That would not be a problem on land, but on a ship, it would require extensive (and expensive) changes to the hull to compensate for the new hydrodynamic profile.

It cost a lot to redesign both the Windjammer Café and the hull form, but it was worth it. The Windjammer Café was an exciting new feature on the original *Sovereign*-class ships. Since then, a Windjammer Café has been included on every Royal Caribbean ship. And, as we learned the ropes, each new incarnation of the room has been better than the last. Today, the Windjammer Café is one of Royal Caribbean's most popular venues.

This was more than a design decision. Going forward, we agreed that we would continue our push for innovation even on sisterships and even if it cost more. At the same time, we committed ourselves to adhere to the cost discipline of not making changes unless there were tangible benefits. This was one of the earliest formal applications of the concept of continuous improvement, which became a mainstay of our culture and a key driver of our long-term success.

In its simplest form, continuous improvement is the process of relentlessly seeking new and better ways to accomplish something.

The key principle is that making something better doesn't imply that the prior arrangement was wrong. It is a permanent mindset that aspires toward becoming better today than we were yesterday and even better tomorrow.

Continuous improvement is hard to ingrain in an organization partially because—by definition—it means that you are never satisfied. A success is never final; it is merely a stepping stone to an even better future. But a true commitment to continuous improvement is critical for an organization to deliver excellence. It's not a technique; it's a mindset. It is a refusal to accept that mediocrity is acceptable.

> **Continuous improvement is not a technique; it's a mindset. It is a refusal to accept that mediocrity is acceptable.**

Continuous improvement also means recognizing that your biggest competitor is often yourself. While listening to your customers is crucial, it's not enough. To achieve true success, you must constantly seek ways to improve even before your customers envision the need.

I had a personal experience that vividly demonstrated the power of continuous improvement. One morning, I woke up with a frozen shoulder, making it painful to raise my arm. My physical therapist assured me it was a common issue and recommended a simple exercise using a pedal exerciser—a compact device resembling a stationary bike but without the frame, seat, or wheels. It consists of two rotating pedals attached to a small resistance mechanism, allowing the user to pedal with their hands. The machine displays a graph tracking my speed and effort.

At first, the machine seemed pointless; my shoulder still hurt, and the pedaling seemed silly. Periodically, the therapist would check the graph, but whenever I asked how fast or hard I should pedal, he simply said, "You'll know."

Eventually, I realized that I was competing with myself. I was constantly pushing myself to beat my last performance as measured by the red bars on the display. Gradually, my performance got better (the little red bars kept climbing), and gradually, my shoulder began to loosen up. Without even realizing it, I was racing myself—and winning. There is no motivation like self-motivation. In short order, my frozen shoulder was history.

This personal experience reinforced another fundamental truth that is critical in an organization's activities: What gets measured gets better. The mere act of collecting the data improves performance even before any decisions are made based on that data. In this case, the therapist didn't need to analyze my pedal exerciser graphs to adjust my treatment. He knew that just showing me the data would push me to pedal harder and faster.

Bastard.

We quickly found many areas of our operations where this lesson could be applied. One early example was our employee bonus program. Like most such programs, it was based exclusively on financial metrics. If our net income improved, the bonuses for employees would increase accordingly. That seemed normal and logical, but we wanted to do more and took a different approach. We expanded the criteria for calculating bonuses to include nonfinancial metrics like safety, employee engagement, guest satisfaction, and energy consumption. The goal was to ensure that everyone saw these as collective responsibilities, not just the domain of departments or specialists.

What gets measured gets better.

At first, the pushback was strong. "Why should my bonus suffer if someone slips on a door sill?" one IT expert asked. An accountant questioned, "What does employee engagement have to do with me? I just keep the books."

But over time, people began to see the power of interconnectedness. Just like in rowing, success required everyone pulling in sync. Simply tracking and sharing these metrics created alignment, driving us to become better, safer, stronger. Once people realized that the goal of each of these metrics was to instill excellence at every level and across the organization, everything clicked. We were all connected, and if each of us was committed to excellence in our job, the entire organization would thrive.

Measuring the WOW proved to be an effective catalyst for delivering the WOW.

ENGAGING DEBATE

As the years passed, debate intensified around our grow-or-die mantra. As the company expanded, more voices began to argue against such rapid growth. They made a simple supply-and-demand argument: If we reduced the supply of ships, we could drive up prices, increasing profitability while reducing risk.

I strongly disagreed with this line of thinking. While we had grown at lightning speed by historical measures, our share of the total vacation market was still miniscule; there was lots of room to grow within this larger market. If our real competitors were hotels and resorts, how would reducing the supply of ships help? Moreover, if we failed to build new ships, we would not be able to develop the kind of innovations that would expand the market and differentiate us from our competition—on land and sea.

This view remained controversial. Conventional wisdom held that even in a noncommodity business like cruising, the general price level was mainly determined by market forces, and the ability of any one company to do better was limited—not zero but limited. After Royal Caribbean went public in 1993, we felt even more pressure from Wall Street to moderate our expenditure on efforts to innovate and differentiate ourselves.

While the pressure to slow down our growth was frustrating, it also had a positive effect: It forced us to critically reexamine our grow-or-die mentality. That scrutiny made us even more confident in our decisions and helped us refine the details.

True alignment depends on informed participation, not blind conformity.

An example of that self-examination happened every time we proposed new ship orders to the board. Each time, Jay Pritzker would reliably ask, "Richard, when will the next ship be one ship too many?" He would then pursue the subject relentlessly, asking question after question to make sure we had done our homework—and no one played devil's advocate better than Jay Pritzker.

Eventually, someone else would start to speak in support of his (apparent) skepticism, and when that happened, Jay would immediately change course 180° and say, "It's a big risk, but I suppose we just have to support Richard on this."

The arguments weren't just about building new and better ships. There was a clear understanding that our future depended on WOWing our guests, not just satisfying them. That kind of differentiation doesn't always come from dramatic innovations. Sometimes, it comes from fixing things that aren't totally broken.

For example, our surveys showed that our guests liked our cabins, but they didn't love our cabins. As we talked more to our loyal guests, it became clear that one issue was the mattress. Our mattresses weren't "bad" . . . but they certainly weren't something to write home about.

We decided to replace our mattresses with the latest models, but the cost to upgrade the entire fleet would be huge. Some suggested we do it gradually to spread the pain, but that would also delay the benefit. If we were doing something to please our guests, we needed to please all our guests, not some this year and some in future years.

If we were going to be true to our goals, we had to act accordingly and we did. One letter I received from a frequent cruiser after the upgrade summed it up nicely. "I've always loved your cruises even though your beds were awful," he said. "I just came back from a cruise with your new mattresses, and I slept like a baby. I now love your cruises unconditionally." Unconditional love. That's worth the price.

SHORTER TERM ACTIONS

We still had an immediate problem. The new owners had paid $550 million for Royal Caribbean. Public shareholders were now paying significantly more to buy our stock. We all understood that such a valuation was more than our past performance justified. They were investing in the opportunity to build on the company's established brand, reputation, and market position, much like purchasing a sapling with the confidence that it would one day grow into a towering tree.

New ships and innovation would pay off in time, but we needed our existing orchard to perform better while our saplings were growing. We needed to take advantage of our growing scale to improve customer demand and operational efficiency.

We had alignment on our North Star, but now we needed to extend that alignment down to much smaller details. The cruise business is incredibly complex and involves hundreds of people making thousands of individual decisions that need to be in harmony. Each person makes his or her decisions without knowing how all the others are making theirs.

That is where alignment proves its worth. Each person needs to make their decision with confidence that everyone else is acting pursuant to a common vision. Such alignment can't simply be dictated from on high. Obedience isn't alignment. Similarly, consensus is not synonymous with alignment.

> **Alignment can't be dictated from on high. Obedience and consensus are not alignment.**

Genuine alignment requires that everyone feels heard and a part of the process—but not that every view is accepted. As Eyal Ofer says, "Everyone gets their say, but not everyone gets their way." The process is not efficient, but it is effective. It builds trust, strengthens commitment, and, most importantly, ensures that when decisions are made, the team moves forward together.

One example related to our onboard casinos. These were operated by a well-respected outside company overseen by our Hotel Department.

While the profits from the casino were acceptable, we needed more than merely "acceptable." We thought there was an opportunity to improve the casinos' performance by operating them ourselves, but the Hotel Department worried about the risk of changing something that was "working fine." Their position was understandable looked at in isolation, but to reach our North Star, every part of the business had to push aggressively toward a common goal.

Incrementalism destroys transformation. If even one area lagged behind, it would disrupt the rhythm of our progress—like a single rower hesitating midstroke, throwing the entire boat off its stride.

It was our responsibility as leaders to both explain the vision of the transformation we were seeking and to insist that the Hotel Department play its part in achieving it. The main job of a leader is to lead.

We took over the casino operations expecting that we could achieve a helpful but not huge improvement. It would be one part of a company-wide program to increase profitability—one cog in the larger profitability engine.

It turned out to be a bigger deal than we had imagined. Once we became actively involved in the management and worked directly with our guests, we realized that there was a lot we could do to make the casinos more attractive and efficient. Today, we make more profit from our casinos every week—and with higher guest satisfaction scores—than we were making annually in 1988. Of course, we are a vastly larger operation, but the scale only explains a fraction of the increase.

The main job of a leader is to lead.

In the years that followed, we internalized many other services, including dining service, culinary operations, housekeeping, beverage, marine operations, and photography. That success boosted our bottom line, but the deeper impact was cultural: It brought us closer to our guests and deepened our understanding of what mattered most to them. That improved understanding of our guests' needs (I don't think of them as *wants*) may well have been one of the most important benefits.

Not all such efforts went smoothly. In some cases, our aspirations didn't meet our capabilities. For example, we thought it would be a piece of cake to run the onboard retail shops, but, boy, were we wrong. We just didn't have the infrastructure or expertise to be successful in this area. When we took it over, sales sank, inventory became chaotic, and guest satisfaction plummeted. With chagrin, we accepted that we didn't have the necessary resources internally and went back to relying on concessionaires for the shops. Not every transformational change will succeed, but you'll never know which ones will unless you take the leap.

> **Not every transformational change will succeed, but you'll never know which ones will unless you take the leap.**

Another big opportunity to improve our performance related to the independent travel advisors (known then as *travel agents*) who booked the bulk of our guests. We paid them commissions of 10 percent, 15 percent, or more. Cutting them out and selling directly to the consumer appeared to be an obvious route to reducing our costs. In fact, the airlines were taking aggressive steps to do just that, and many people were encouraging us to do the same.

WHAT DRESSES AND CRUISES HAVE IN COMMON

While this issue was being debated in 1991, I went shopping with my 14-year-old daughter, Sara, to buy her a dress. Sara assumed that I knew what to do, but she was unduly optimistic. It quickly became clear that I was out of my depth—like I'd stepped into the *Twilight Zone*.

Thankfully, a salesperson came over and began to ask a series of practical questions. What's the occasion for the dress? How fancy? What colors? What lengths? I never knew that so much information was required just to buy a simple dress.

Pretty soon, though, she had helped us identify a category of dress, narrowed it down to a few options, and finally, helped us find a front-runner. She even offered suggestions for a scarf and shoes. In my basic training days, we once had to crawl through a muddy field at night under barbed wire while tracer bullets zipped overhead. That was definitely a less traumatic experience for me than shopping for a dress with my teenage daughter.

Without the salesperson's help, I would not have been able to make the most basic choices. Instead, in her capable hands, my teenage daughter left the store happy. She even thanked me. My teenage daughter actually thanked me!

I realized that cruisers often felt the same way I did in that store: overwhelmed. To book a cruise, you have to choose which port to sail from, but what's the significance of one port over another? Why pick Miami versus Fort Lauderdale? Some cruise lines cater to a specific clientele—older guests, families, or couples. On Royal Caribbean's cruises in China, the language is Mandarin. Imagine booking that by accident. The travel advisor can provide valuable advice that helps people make informed decisions about a cruise instead of another vacation.

The role of the travel advisor was something that Bob Dickinson, then Carnival's head of sales and marketing (and subsequently Carnival brand president), understood better than we did. Continuous improvement includes learning from others, and we studied Bob from a distance, often asking travel advisors what they appreciated about his approach. In this way, we got a free master class in winning the support of travel advisors.

The lesson for me was that when buying a dress or a cruise, the right guide can make all the difference.

INSPIRING OURSELVES

Our goal with all these changes in the 1990s was to grow, and grow we did. Within a decade, our formerly little cruise line represented 25 percent of the total cruise business, behind only Carnival, which had almost 50 percent. Royal Caribbean was now one of the two dominant players, large enough to be an influential presence in the market. More importantly, we were now big enough to afford the investments required for innovating in everything from technology to management systems, hiring the best people, and designing and building bigger and better ships.

As part the process, we decided that we needed to reemphasize a few key behaviors to crew members and especially to new crew members. We wanted an easy phrase and decided to call it *GOLD Anchor Standards* (tying into our crown-and-anchor logo). For the acronym GOLD, we had G for *Greet the guest*, O for *Own the problem*, and L for *Look the part*.

But we were stuck on the D until someone said that D could be *Deliver the WOW*. That was the moment the title of this book was born. The phrase began as the last letter of our GOLD Anchor Standards acronym, but it would soon come first in epitomizing all that we stood for, all that we did.

Our crown-and-anchor logo provided the perfect visual anchor. Delivering the WOW became more than a rallying cry; it defined our

The crown-and-anchor logo.

identity and purpose. Delivering the WOW to our guests became our passion, and that passion became our culture.

EXPANSION

Given that our objective was to become competitive in the broader vacation market, it was obviously important that we expand our ecosystem of products. The company had started with a single brand—originally called Royal Caribbean Cruise Line—and now started looking for other cruise brands that would enable us to offer a broader range of products.

In 1997, we acquired Celebrity Cruises, which had established itself as a premium brand offering upscale experiences with a focus on elevated culinary offerings. In 2006, we acquired Pullmantur, which offered budget cruises targeted to Spanish-speaking travelers from Spain and Latin America. In 2008, we formed TUI Cruises in partnership with TUI AG to offer quality cruises to Germans and German-speaking people. In 2018, we acquired Silversea Cruises, an ultra-luxury cruise brand appealing mainly to American and European guests. And in 2019, we inked a deal to add Hapag-Lloyd Cruises into TUI Cruises to offer upscale German cruises.

All of these acquisitions were consistent with our strategy of broadening our appeal to be competitive in the broader vacation market. By having multiple brands, it enabled us to offer a larger ecosystem of products.

One downside of having different brands is the confusion over company names. I will use the same convention here that Royal Caribbean Group uses in its own communications.

- *Royal Caribbean Group* refers to the entire company including all the brands.
- *Royal Caribbean* normally refers to the brand Royal Caribbean, but in this book, I have sometimes gotten lazy and

used the term to refer to the whole group. If so, the context normally makes the intent clear.

- *Celebrity, TUI Cruises, Silversea, Pullmantur,* and *Hapag-Lloyd* refer to the respective brands.

In the years that followed, we did grow. We grew fast, but what mattered most wasn't how many ships we added, or how many guests we served—it was how we grew as a company, and as people. We grew by taking chances. We grew by listening. We grew by caring deeply—sometimes unreasonably—about getting things right.

The result is a culture that supports and sustains the Royal Caribbean Group. Not every decision we made was perfect. But our compass never wavered. It is that culture which drives our success. Not our ships or our marketing programs or our culinary offerings.

It is our culture.

A PERSONAL REFLECTION

I can't look back on this period without thinking about how lucky I am.

I had the amazing support of family, friends, and awesome colleagues. But during this particular chapter of my journey, I was especially blessed to have the mentorship, the support—and yes, the love—of three extraordinary men: Arne Wilhelmsen, Jay Pritzker, and Sammy Ofer. These three believed in me and believed in the opportunity to make a difference.

They were engaged, constructive, and determined. Their vision, their passion, and their good sense motivated and inspired me. They pushed me to be the best I could be, and they guided me on that path. I remember one time, when I had given a particularly long-winded explanation of something, Jay said, "Richard, if we can't get you to talk less, could you possibly talk faster?"

All three have now passed. I miss them more than I know how to express.

But my luck has stayed with me. Jay's and Sammy's sons—Tom and Eyal—were involved from the very beginning. Arne's son, Alex, joined slightly later. All three have become not only valued partners but also trusted friends. They bring their own wisdom and energy, but they also carry forward their fathers' spirit—with grace, courage, and heart.

I am incredibly lucky to have them in my life. I wish I had all six. But I am grateful beyond words to have these three—and the lasting memory of their fathers.

KEY TAKEAWAYS

- Decisiveness and strategic foresight are critical to growth; instead of waiting for proof of demand, Royal Caribbean embraced an aggressive strategy, betting on where the market was heading rather than where it had been.
- What gets measured, gets better; tracking performance data alone can drive progress.
- Alignment is essential for complex growth; genuine organizational alignment isn't about obedience or consensus but ensuring that everyone understands and supports a shared vision.
- With a clear North Star in place, execution has to be intentional and unwavering; success depends on unrelenting pursuit of the goal rather than settling for incremental changes.

All hands on deck:

Hands is an old term for sailors or crew members. In a storm or other emergency, the captain would shout, "All hands on deck!" That meant everyone had to drop whatever they were doing and come up to the main deck to help out. These days, work on ships happens below deck, but the phrase stuck around. Now, people use it in all kinds of situations—not just on ships. If something big is happening and everyone's help is needed, "All hands on deck!" means everyone needs to help address the issue.

5

It's the People, It's the People, It's the People

If you are reading this book, you have probably experienced our cruises and felt the WOW. And you have probably met the amazing people who deliver that WOW, whether they work on the ship serving grande lattes with a sprinkle of cinnamon or in the office designing a cabana for our next Perfect Day location.

WOW moments on board aren't always grand gestures. More often, they're found in the small, meaningful touches—a warm smile that makes you feel instantly at home, a crew member who kneels down to talk to your child at eye level, the graceful way a meal is presented like it was made just for you. It's in how our crew shows up every day—with heart, joy, and an unwavering commitment to making each guest feel special.

Even when no one's watching, their passion shines through. These quiet acts of care, repeated thousands of times a day, are what turn a voyage into something unforgettable. They're the everyday WOWs that make guests feel seen, cherished, and part of something magical.

That's the spirit—the passion—that sets our culture apart.

Ironically, some of the most powerful reminders of how great our crew members truly are come not from glowing reviews, but from guests who did not enjoy their cruise. I've received my share of letters from angry guests (yes, not everyone has a perfect cruise!) but even those letters often look like this:

```
Dear Mr. Fain,

You are an idiot. Your company
is terrible.

On our cruise, this went wrong
and that went wrong. Everything
was awful.

However, George, my cabin
steward, was wonderful. And
Ana, our waiter, was fantastic.
Don't blame them!

                    Sincerely,
                A furious guest
```

Even in their anger, even when every other part of their experience failed, our frustrated guests often recognize how exceptional our individual crew members are. Ana and George do us proud, and they are what makes our cruises so special.

They are the ones who brighten my cabin with towel animals. They are the ones who remember not only my name but also my preference in drinks. They are the ones who design the smallest detail on our ships. Most importantly, they are the ones who constantly smile, who show that they care. The WOW is not just the service; it's the unmistakable sincerity.

One of the great joys of my role over these 33 years is the warm feeling I get from working with such a group of passionate, talented, and determined individuals. I frequently ask myself how we find so many amazing people or how we transform so many ordinary people into superheroes.

The people shape the culture, and the culture helps shape the people.

Over decades of pondering the same question, I have learned we have to do both. The people shape the culture, and the culture helps shape the people.

HOW DO WE ATTRACT SO MANY AMAZING PEOPLE?

The best people can usually choose where they want to work. To attract them, we need to be the employer of choice, so if they get a similar offer from two companies, they will think, *I prefer the one from Royal Caribbean Group. That's where I want to work.*

Getting that kind of reputation is hard, of course, but just as we need to be intentional to build the most innovative ships, we need to be intentional to be the employer of choice. We can't be tentative; we need to focus on that objective and make sure that every action, every decision furthers that goal.

We have to WOW our people just like we have to WOW our guests. And, like the design of our ships, it requires an unwavering commitment and a touch of magic to make it happen. For example, when computer tablets were relatively new, we saw an opportunity to address one of the most painful challenges our crew members face—the hardship of long months away from their loved ones. We decided to give every crew member an iPad or tablet, which they could use for whatever purpose they wished, including video calls home. I was certain it would be very impactful. We bought 50,000 tablets and started handing them out.

> **Delivering the WOW to your people requires unwavering commitment and a touch of magic.**

It turned out it was impactful, but not in the way I had expected. While the crew loved the idea, many already had something similar. As a result, the new tablets weren't as transformational as I had hoped.

But it did reflect who we were and influenced how we were viewed. A year or so later, I was interviewing a candidate for a senior operations role. I asked him why he was interested in the job, and he replied that he had heard about the tablets and said to himself, *That's the kind of company I want to work for.*

In the end, the impact wasn't about the technology; it was about the message it sent.

TRANSFORMING ORDINARY PEOPLE INTO SUPERHEROES

The best learning does not come from formal training programs but rather from existing employees instilling the company's culture in the next generation. Good training can teach the mechanics, but delivering the WOW requires magic, and that can't be taught; it can only be demonstrated by example.

Of course, we have good training programs, but enthusiasm can't be taught; insatiability can't be taught. One absorbs that through working with people who know and live the culture. For that reason, we work hard to fill jobs from within. Nationally, only about a quarter of jobs are filled from within, but at Royal Caribbean's offices, the proportion exceeds 40 percent and on the ships, it reaches nearly 80 percent.

This strong focus on internal promotion both reflects our culture and actively reinforces it. One result is the average tenure of our senior officers now exceeds 15 years, which means they have absorbed the company culture until they can live it, develop it further, and teach it to others.

And when we do bring in new talent, we seek those with a willingness or ability to work in an environment with our level of passion and insatiability. We want people who are never satisfied with what is, always striving for what can be. It is easier to find someone who has the necessary skills than it is to find someone who has the necessary attitudes. You can't teach this; it needs to be a part of the culture that is absorbed.

One letter I received from a guest on *Quantum of the Seas* really summed it up nicely. She told me that her husband had suffered a heart attack, and, while the medical team worked to stabilize him, their cabin steward stayed by her side. The steward didn't do anything except be present and offer comfort. The guest's words, which have stayed with me ever since, were simple but evocative, "The doctors had all the knowledge and training, but my steward had the heart and the caring; she was just as important to my recovery as the doctors were to his."

We try to hire exceptional people capable of excellence; people who have the confidence to act on their own but not the arrogance to believe that only they know what works best. The company needs a diversity of voices like we had in the steering committee, each with a willingness at times to step outside their formal roles and challenge conventional wisdom.

THE DEMANDS—AND REWARDS—OF EXCELLENCE

Working for Royal Caribbean is not easy, but it is deeply rewarding. Delivering the WOW provides our people with a strong sense of purpose and pride in their work. That passion is fulfilling, but it is also demanding.

Shipboard work is tough: long hours, demanding jobs, months away from loved ones. Shoreside work is also difficult. Regardless of where you work, excellence is the floor expectation, not the ceiling. The culture of continuous improvement means your boss is never satisfied. Constantly trying to do everything better, faster, smarter is demanding. These are not conventional 9-to-5 jobs; they're roles for people who thrive on making an impact.

This was brought home to me in a very tangible way when two different employees on separate occasions spoke to me about their experience. Both had worked previously in the public sector, one in a charitable organization and one in government. Both said that they left their public jobs reluctantly, driven by a need for better compensation. They felt good about their public service but were willing to give up that sense of purpose for a bigger paycheck. Now, to their surprise, they felt they had the best of both worlds. They felt a sense of purpose *and* still got a nice paycheck.

Of course, not everyone feels that way. Retaining top talent means keeping those who excel, but it also means parting ways with those who aren't the right fit. I use the word *fit* rather than *performance* intentionally. In many organizations, a termination is a bit like a traditional divorce—structured in a manner that forces people to find fault until they hate each other. Too often, the result is a vicious circle where both the senior person and the junior person feel compelled to highlight the other's failures. Protecting employees from bad bosses is important, but at leadership levels, no-fault separation is usually more constructive than an adversarial process.

> **The real issue is fit, not fitness.**

The real issue is usually fit, not fitness.

I saw a vivid example of this when we shifted two senior executives to new roles. In the morning, one of them came to me and said his new second-in-command, Sam, was useless and that he would like to replace him with Kevin, his former number two. In the afternoon, the other executive said exactly the opposite: Kevin was useless, and she wanted to replace him with Sam. Obviously, Kevin and Sam couldn't simultaneously be useless and fantastic. The issue wasn't their ability; it was their chemistry with new leaders. Sam and Kevin swapped positions, and it worked out very well. The issue wasn't performance; it was fit.

INSTILLING OUR CULTURE

Even with the best people, supporting and encouraging a culture of WOW requires constant effort. The real education takes place outside the classroom, through everyday osmosis. There is no simple list of rules, no how-to manual, no formula. Instead, there are habits, practices, and styles of communication that are constantly reinforced. There is experience. And there is the power of WOW.

One way we encourage that is cross-fertilization. As part of a normal career path, we actively move employees from department to department to broaden their perspective and deepen their understanding of the business. Michael Bayley, now president and CEO of the Royal Caribbean brand, started on board as a purser. He later moved ashore and had stints in human resources, marketing, onboard revenue, and hotel operations. Laura Hodges Bethge, president of the Celebrity Cruises brand, started as an accessibility expert and later spent time in sales, finance, purchasing, operations, and investor relations. Jason Liberty started as our internal auditor but later was responsible for finance, technology, supply chain, and the Silversea brand.

Across the organization, we make a deliberate effort to rotate talent across functions to break down silos and hopefully inspire fresh thinking. This kind of broad experience not only adds to their skill sets, but it also encourages everyone to weigh in on virtually any topic because the mystique of specialized knowledge isn't there. Because of this cross-fertilization, the person across the table from you is more likely to challenge you (or at least argue with you) because they are likely to have been in your seat previously. It makes the discussion more constructive, because more voices are empowered and qualified to challenge.

LIFE AT SEA

There are unique considerations that are relevant to working on a cruise ship, and these factors need special attention.

Our crew members come from all over the world; only about 10 percent are American. This means they are away from their family for long stretches, have distinct working habits and cultural norms, enjoy diverse foods, speak different native languages, etc. And yet, once they are on board one of our ships, they work together seamlessly. They are the most visible embodiment of the culture of delivering the WOW, and I couldn't be more in awe of them.

The most critical element to attract the best talent is being their employer of choice. Our reputation is a key element of that, but dedication plays a role here too. One element of that is using data to help us improve. One university provost I know has a screen saver that says,

$$\sum_{i=0}^{\infty} \text{Anecdotes} \neq \text{Data},$$

which translates for nonacademics to "the sum of an infinite number of anecdotes is still not data."

To avoid being misled by a series of anecdotes, we rely on the same kind of polling data that we use to ensure that our guests are happy. And we use that data as part of our continuous improvement focus to constantly address issues on our employees' minds. This is one of the reasons that employee turnover is surprisingly low, especially after their first year. The data really drives change. It tells us that providing food that feels like home is critically important. We even hire cruise directors for the crew. The job of the crew cruise director is very similar to the job of the guest cruise director—to arrange activities, entertainment, and chances to socialize.

We also redesigned our crew cabins and crew policies to better address their quality of life. Our ships have evolved from the previously standard four-person cabins for the junior ranks to a maximum of two in a room in the 1990s. More recently, we switched to more single-share cabins; private cabins that share a bathroom.

One interesting change from many years ago pertains to romantic relationships between crew members. Historically, we discouraged such arrangements and even separated couples onto different ships. Fortunately, attitudes have changed, and now we work diligently to align the schedules of romantic partners and even adjust their living quarters to accommodate. Times change and so must we.

SPEAKING UP AND LISTENING WELL

With over 100,000 employees, we are also conscious that there will, unfortunately, be those who abuse the system and violate our policies. They may be small in number, but they can cause a disproportionate amount of harm to our people and to our culture. If employees are uncomfortable, if they are harassed, if they see or experience misconduct, then their morale will suffer. They will lose the pride and enthusiasm that is their hallmark.

There is no perfect answer to this, but working to ensure that every employee has a reliable way to voice concerns is key. Like many companies, we implemented an employee hotline where people can report problems anonymously. Most importantly, we make sure that every call is treated with the importance it deserves, engaging people from outside the chain of command and across the organization—an all-hands-on-deck effort. We also provide updates to the caller using a code that enables them to get an update on their report while maintaining anonymity.

Listening—really listening—is essential at every level of the organization. Whether it's creating safe, anonymous channels for employees to report misconduct or understanding what our guests need before they ever step on board, the ability to tune in and respond thoughtfully makes all the difference.

I received a pointed lesson to that effect in the early 1990s when we tried to improve our pre-booking communications.

MANNING THE PHONES—AND LEARNING LESSONS

We realized that not many of us in management really understood much about the workings of our reservation call centers. These call centers were our primary pre-cruise connection with our guests and advisors. We decided that requiring every officer of the company to spend a day on the telephone lines would help us understand. What an eye-opener.

When it was my turn, it quickly became obvious how much training I lacked. They positioned me with Craig, who was very experienced. Craig listened to every call and passed me notes with the answers. I thought I was pretty knowledgeable about our business, but I quickly realized how little I knew when Craig used up his first notepad and started on another.

Whenever a caller asked something too complex for a quick note, I had to say, "Can you hold a minute please while I check on that?" The first time that happened, Craig stopped me. He pointed out that after asking the caller if they minded holding, I put them on hold without waiting for their answer. That's a no-no. He said I should always wait for them to confirm before I pushed the hold button. It was such a simple but meaningful act of politeness, but I had never thought about it. Simple politeness matters.

As the day wore on, I gained a better appreciation of just how complex the job of a reservationist really was. They were expected to know such a vast array of details about an ever-expanding list of ships, destinations, and policies. It was dizzying and I began to get a more vivid sense of the needs of the potential customer, how the experience of the cruise came across on a call, and the challenges of the reservationist's job.

That day on the phones reinforced my understanding of the importance of every interaction between the company and the guest. Many years later, that experience served me in another way. It motivated and informed my eagerness to use technology to simplify the mechanical processes for booking and boarding a ship.

By the way, if you called our phone line in April of 1993 and talked to someone named Ricardo who seemed bewildered, please accept my belated apology.

CREW DINNERS

That day in the call center reminded us of how easy it is to lose sight of what frontline employees go through every day, but the risk of misunderstanding is even bigger between employees in the office on land and those on the ships. Shipboard employees often felt the office didn't understand them, and the office people felt the same about the shipboard people.

In order to bridge that divide, we came up with the idea that office employees and senior ship's officers should occasionally serve the crew a dinner on board. It sounded simple—until we learned how hard it really is.

The exercise produced insights before the first meal even began. I was assigned to be a waiter; the captain was a wine steward; and Colleen, my wife, was to be one of the people who cleared the tables, what was known as a *busboy*. I was used to that word, but when I heard Colleen called it, I became especially aware that she was not a boy. (Actually,

I was aware of that already.) She was a woman, and the term *busboy* was silly and undignified. When we looked at it, we realized that quite a few onboard titles were unnecessarily gender-specific or demeaning. We went on to rename that role *assistant waiter* and to improve our language more generally.

The intention was for us to deliver the same experience as the dining service team, but a real Royal Caribbean dinner turned out to be too hard for us executives and ship's officers. The meals were usually simplified to only two choices for appetizer, two for main dish, and two for dessert. Even then, the insurance company set limits on what untrained waitstaff could do; we couldn't serve soup, for example, because we might spill it and injure someone.

Delivering dinner to the crew. I still had the mustache.

On one of these dinners, a group of maître d's chose to sit at the captain's table with me as their waiter, the captain as their wine steward, and the hotel director as their head waiter. The group came to the dining room dressed in formal wear on top and Hawaiian shorts and tennis shoes below. I still remember delivering the first course, shrimp cocktail. Right away, I got a complaint from one of my guests pretending to be an irate diner.

"There are five shrimps on this plate," he said. "I've cruised with you 20 times, and there are always six shrimps in the shrimp cocktail."

"Oh, terribly sorry, sir," I said. "Let me get you some more shrimp."

"No!" he shouted. "You're missing the point. Your standards are falling, and it's terrible. I want to speak to someone in charge."

I brought over the head waiter (aka the hotel director). He listened to this "angry" guest, and together, we apologized for his missing sixth shrimp. But he wasn't letting us off easy. He continued to complain at length about his missing shrimp and how "disappointed" he was. He and his tablemates clearly enjoyed making us squirm, but they also gave us a better understanding of the kinds of issues they face every day.

After we served the meal, the diners left, and we waiters-for-a-night sat down, exhausted. Then one of the head waiters spoke into a microphone, saying, "Okay, people! Time to get ready for second seating!" There was no second seating for this crew dinner (whew) but the announcement served as a poignant reminder of how demanding this job was. We could barely perform a small part of what they did every day.

Understanding the people in your organization improves dialogue, collaboration, and empathy.

The result of this exercise, which we repeated on different ships for many years, was that people in the office became more understanding of people on the ship, and there was more of a bond all around. The practice served to improve dialogue, collaboration, and empathy between the office and ship staff and led to better ideas and solutions for the company.

CULTURAL FIT

The first step in our hiring process is, of course, to satisfy ourselves that the candidate has the right skill and experience for the job they are being recruited for. But that's the easy part. The real challenge is whether the person will fit culturally into the fabric of our company.

When I interview candidates, I rarely ask them about their technical qualifications, which I assume has already been covered in previous interviews. Instead, I like to talk about who they are and what drives them. Besides, it's much more fun to talk about their military career or hobbies or whatever.

In 2005, I hurt my back and spent two days lying in bed, moaning. (Back pains are the worst.) Our head of HR called and asked me to meet that evening with a candidate named Jason Liberty for the head of Internal Audit. He sympathized with my back pain (or claimed to) and said that Jason was on the cusp of being named a partner at KPMG (one of the Big Four accounting firms), and that we needed to act fast if we wanted to win him over.

This was an important move for us and, as miserable as I was, our HR director did the right thing to insist I meet Jason. Internal Audit was then seen as a policing function, but we wanted it to play a more proactive, advisory role. As we often do, we decided to emphasize the new mandate by changing the department name from *Internal Audit* to *Audit and Advisory Services*.

Jason's background was excellent; he had even done successful consulting work for us. But KPMG would fight to keep him. We met in my library at home, and it was quickly apparent that Jason would be a great choice if we could land him.

We didn't talk much about his work at KPMG or his work consulting for us or the new role. Instead, we talked about his life—his experiences, his values, and even his exercise program. I hadn't exercised since high school, so I was fascinated by his routine of swimming three kilometers four days a week at 5:30 a.m. I was impressed not just by his physical dedication but by the discipline and commitment it reflected.

I also appreciated the collaborative spirit he conveyed and gave him extra marks for not mentioning the partnership that I knew KPMG was dangling in front of him.

I was impressed by that afternoon interview, and we offered him the job. We soon got an early indication of his capabilities. The first project he undertook was to develop an enterprise risk assessment project—a new SEC requirement. While many companies treated it as a check-the-box exercise, Jason took it on with resolve. After he presented the results to our audit committee, two members asked me if they could share it with other boards they served on.

I didn't imagine at the time that, 20 years later, Jason would become CEO of the company. And it all started with a conversation, not about his résumé but about who he was.

BEING PART OF SOMEONE'S DREAM

I am so overwhelmingly proud of the joy that our people produce for our guests. I never cease to be amazed with how deep it runs and how genuinely constructive it is. There have been many specific times when this is brought home to me, but two stand out.

The first was in 1999, when Turkey was hit with a magnitude 7.4 quake. Thousands died, and the devastation was horrific. We donated to the relief fund and then said that if any crew member wanted to contribute, we would match their donation. I was not surprised that many crew members chose to make donations, but I was shocked that the largest single group of contributors were our Greek crew members. Greece and Turkey are traditional enemies, and the fact that our Greek crew would be so supportive of their Turkish coworkers spoke volumes about the culture on board.

My other experience was a time when I was on board *Oasis* for some meetings during a changeover day. The old guests had just left, and the new ones hadn't yet boarded. My meeting was later in the day, so I spent some time wandering around the ship. In one of the sculleries, I said hello to a Jamaican crew member who was assiduously cleaning pots and pans.

"Oh, Mr. Richard," he said. "It's so nice to see you again. We met when I was on *Song of America*, in 1996." I said that was many years ago, and he said, "I was thinking of coming to see you in your office. I'm retiring from Royal Caribbean in April after 22 years, and I wanted to tell you."

"Oh, my goodness," I said. "Why is that?"

He said, "I've done well here, and the money I earned enabled me to put my daughter through school. I'm so proud of her. She did well and started her own business. When I go home on vacation, I help her with it, but now the business is growing so fast she needs me full time. So, I have to leave, but I didn't want anyone to think that I was unhappy with the company. Now that you're here, I can tell you face to face, and I hope you understand."

> It is hard to overstate the power of concerted action to accomplish a clear goal.

I was gobsmacked, at a total loss for words, and emotionally touched. He was so proud of all that he and his daughter had achieved. He valued his time with the company. And he knew we valued him. What more could anyone hope for than to be part of someone's dream?

THE INCREDIBLE POWER—AND LIMITS— OF RELATIONSHIPS

No company thrives on internal culture alone. Some of our most decisive wins—and our narrowest escapes—have come from the strength of relationships outside our own walls. Lenders, shipyards, travel advisors, and even former employees have stood with us in moments when we needed them, when many would have walked away.

These bonds don't just happen because you're polite or professional.

They require the same intentionality we've discussed throughout this book—and often more.

External relationships are less automatic than the ones inside your company, and it's easy to treat them as one-off transactions. The real value comes from finding reasons to connect, building trust before you need it, and staying in touch whether times are good or bad. Lenders, for example, should hear from you when things are going well, not only when you're asking for help. Regular communication builds trust as well as friendships.

That lesson was brought home to me one night when our eldest daughter called us at 2:00 a.m. The phone in the middle of the night made my heart jump; these are the calls every parent dreads. She explained the problem and—happily—it was resolved before morning. She was apologetic about disturbing us, but we told her that her call was really a gift. We now knew that she would call in an emergency; that assurance was a blessing that would save us endless worry.

At Royal Caribbean, we have seen the strengths of relationships as well as the limits. During crises like 9/11 and COVID, our banks stood by us and were extremely supportive. But there are also limits. During the Great Recession, the government pressured all banks to act more conservatively. This classic example of "closing of the barn door after the horse has bolted" had the effect of exacerbating an already difficult situation. Our lenders were less helpful than we expected, but even while they were dealing with their own pressures, our relationships helped us avoid the worst impacts.

Relationships with shipyards have demonstrated a different kind of partnership—one rooted in shared creativity and decades of trust. Our people work incredibly hard to innovate with new ideas and new designs, but none of them would have been possible on our own. In every case, our shipyard partners in Finland, France, and Germany have applied the same passion, the same determination and the same commitment to excellence. While we get the ultimate credit (or blame), none of it would have been possible without their active participation and commitment.

We sign contracts for each new ship, but in my 33 years, I have never had occasion to refer to a shipbuilding contract or even look at a copy after it was signed. We had something more than a piece of paper—we had a shared mission of building something special . . . something that would make a difference. Our partners honored that mission far better than any legal document.

These are not just vendors; they are partners in the truest sense. During the building of *Voyager*, we were concerned that construction progress was behind schedule. Harri and I visited the yard in Turku and toured the partially built ship with the yard management.

The yard's policy at the time was to stop all outdoor work if the temperature dropped below minus 20°C. The temperature on this day was a balmy minus 14°C. Despite wearing every layer I owned, the cold cut straight and I couldn't stop shivering. The yard workers were just as bundled with warming tents and hot toddies, but we all knew that no one could be productive in that cold.

It was the yard's responsibility to get the ship built on time, but we agreed that we would contribute to the cost of heating the ship because we viewed ourselves as partners, not just customers. Naturally, things are never simple—the local electrical grid didn't have enough capacity to heat a massive cruise ship and simultaneously power up every sauna in town each afternoon. The solution was pure partnership—and a little diplomacy. We agreed to heat the ship until 3 p.m., then shut the heat down so the Finns could have their beloved saunas (a non-negotiable national priority). At midnight, they would restart the heating so the ship would be toasty by morning. Without a strong relationship with the yard, that compromise would never have happened.

Just as our lenders faced issues following the Great Recession, our shipyards faced problems during and after COVID as the contended with global supply shortages, inflationary pressures, etc. Our ability to work with them to address such issues reflected the same cooperative spirit that has proven so impactful in all our relationships.

And it's not just Finland. For example, our work in France has spanned decades and personalities, from Alain Grill's promise to give us a "French touch" to Laurent Castaing's modern-day enthusiasm for exceptional design changes that would have tested the patience of Job. Their willingness to embrace ideas—their commitment to developing new concepts that pushed themselves and us to new levels—is a direct reflection of trust built over years of collaboration.

The list goes on. Travel advisors feed us a flow of guests as well as supportive advice. Experts in myriad subjects like finance, engineering, design, and systems all work closely with us to constantly push the envelope.

These relationships—too many to name—are just as important to our success as the trust we build with our internal people. The key is intentionality. It has to be a cultural norm . . . every employee from the leadership on down needs to feel the importance of developing and nurturing these relationships. Everyone must invest in relationships—deliberately and methodically—just as you do with employees and even marriages.

ALIGNMENT AROUND DEFINED GOALS

I keep emphasizing the importance of collaboration and energetic debate as central drivers of achieving alignment. But, once the direction has been defined, it is crucial to communicate it effectively to our large and diverse workforce. Getting all Royal Caribbean Group employees to pull in the same direction is a lot more challenging than getting all the rowers in a racing scull to row in sync.

One of the most successful ways we do that at Royal Caribbean is to define a set of goals or objectives that everyone feels is relevant to them and give it a name. It is hard to overstate the power of concerted action to accomplish a clear goal and the value of encapsulating that goal with an aspirational name. It provides a clear and unambiguous North Star for everyone to rally around.

For example, in 2014, we believed that the Royal Caribbean Group was on the cusp of a dramatic turn.

Our *Oasis*-class ships were producing amazing results—for our guests (with satisfaction ratings 10 points above our previous peak), for our investors (with unprecedented occupancy and pricing), and for our crew (with record engagement scores). Our Celebrity brand was gaining momentum with the success of the *Solstice*-class ships and the order of *Edge* class. At the same time, our technology initiatives were finally bearing fruit, improving both operational efficiency and guest experience. Even the external environment was cooperating as the industry recovered from the severe challenges posed by the Great Recession and the disruption following the *Costa Concordia* tragedy.

With all these things going in the right direction, we were ready to roll.

We were positioned to achieve transformational results, but we also knew that it would take a focused, collective effort to reach the goal. If everyone aligned around that target, nothing could stop us. But getting every office, every ship, and every employee to focus on the same goal was a big challenge. People throughout the organization were having to make literally thousands of decisions every day that would make or break our ambition.

DOUBLE-DOUBLE

To coalesce that effort, we created a program called Double-Double. Its goal was to double our earnings per share (EPS) and achieve a double-digit return on invested capital (ROIC) within three years.

These were ambitious goals, but we believed they were achievable if everyone knew and understood the targets. For example, a person in technical purchasing knew that they couldn't accomplish the goal alone, but they knew that their decisions impacted the goal. They could make a difference if they understood what the entire company was heading toward.

EXCELLENCE INCLUDES COST CONSCIOUSNESS

A common but unspoken belief we had to overcome was the idea that operational excellence necessarily comes at the expense of cost control. Our goal of operational excellence was seen by some to be inconsistent with our goal of cost excellence. One of the goals of the Double-Double program was to disprove that thinking—and it succeeded. Today, we are delivering outstanding products while maintaining cost efficiency that ranks among the best in the industry. Excellence in performance and excellence in cost can go hand in hand.

MAKING THE ABSTRACT CONCRETE

In fact, many of our employees didn't even know what EPS and ROIC stood for. But the setting of an overall corporate goal—Double-Double—helped align them with our corporate North Star.

And it worked—beautifully.

We didn't just meet our Double-Double targets; we crushed them. Earnings more than doubled and returns on investment rose sharply. Just as importantly, the team accomplished all this while increasing employee engagement and without sacrificing future growth.

SAYING THANK YOU IS IMPORTANT, TOO

On January 24, 2018, we announced our financial results for the year 2017 showing that we had achieved our Double-Double targets.

Simultaneous with that announcement, we declared that the company was issuing a *Thank You, Thank You Bonus* to the people who had made it happen. The bonus totaled $80 million, and it was given to all employees—full-time and part-time, domestic and overseas—except corporate officers.

Every employee received an equity award equal to 5 percent of their salary vesting over three years. In addition, we contributed to the Crew Welfare Fund, which enhances crew recreational areas.

Personally, I believe the fact that it was given not as an incentive—we had never even hinted at such a bonus—but purely as a gesture of appreciation made it all the more impactful. I also liked the duplication in the name of the bonus, picking up the duplication in the name of the program.

In the end, the power of a group of motivated people pursuing a common goal is awesome to behold. Great ships, effective strategies, and advanced systems all matter—but they are just tools. It's our people who wield them, our people who inspire belief, and our people who deliver the WOW.

A REMINDER

I was reminded of this mantra during a conversation with Alex Wilhelmsen during the inaugural of one of our newest ships.

Alex is now one of our longest serving directors, but he was only two years old when his father, Arne, decided to become one of the three founding owners of the company and 23 when his father partnered with the Pritzkers and Ofers to buy out the other original investors.

We were talking about what truly sets Royal Caribbean apart, and Alex said, "You can build the most beautiful ship in the world, but if the crew on board aren't extraordinary, no one will remember the chandeliers or the slides. They'll remember how they were treated." I've heard versions of this before—but coming from someone whose life has mirrored the company's journey, it resonated strongly.

KEY TAKEAWAYS

- A strong culture sets expectations, and that same culture helps encourage and support the people who bring it to life and deliver the WOW.

- Competitive compensation is necessary but not sufficient; employees stay when they find meaning in their work and feel they are making a difference.

- Success in an organization requires alignment, not just performance; a no-fault approach to leadership transitions reduces toxicity and ensures better team dynamics.

- Rotating employees through different roles enhances skill sets, breaks down silos, and fosters a culture of challenge and continuous improvement.

Feeling blue:

In maritime tradition, when a ship's captain died at sea, the crew would fly blue flags and paint a blue stripe along its hull. Over time, this symbolism made its way into common language, and *feeling blue* became a phrase used to describe sadness or depression.

6

What the Hell?!

For every WOW moment we create, there's a WHOA moment we have to avoid or manage.

Murphy's Law says that anything that can go wrong will go wrong. The corollary for our business is what I now postulate as "The Maritime Megaphone Multiplier": *Anything that goes wrong at sea gets four times the coverage as the same event on land.*

Ships at sea have to deal with a number of issues that land-based businesses don't have to worry about, but the differences also give our ships certain advantages over land-based activities. For example, heart attacks are just as much a concern at sea as on land, but at sea, a doctor is much closer than on land. As a result, your chances of immediately surviving a heart attack at sea are much better than they would be on land. Fire is also a concern in both environments, but cruise ships control their own safety systems rather than rely on the local fire department. As a result, their equipment is often purpose-built for their particular environment and can be more sophisticated and more targeted.

"What the Hell?!" moments—the glitches, breakdowns, and screw-ups that plague any human endeavor— are fertile ground for learning. Continuous improvement helps us to innovate in this area as well. How we react—and what we learn—from mistakes or disasters says everything about our culture.

RUNNING AGROUND OFF ST. MAARTEN

The crisis that unfolded aboard the *Monarch of the Seas* on December 15, 1998, began with a simple medical emergency: A guest had a heart attack. The captain returned the ship to the island of St. Maarten so the guest could be hospitalized.

Once the guest had safely disembarked and the ship left the harbor, the captain—suffering from a nasty cold—handed navigational command to his second officer and retired to his cabin.

Just outside the harbor, there is a reef called the Proselyte Reef, which is a popular dive site during the day. At night, it has a lighted navigation buoy to warn sailors to avoid it. Unfortunately, the second officer focused on the lighted buoy, but didn't check the nautical charts. Even more unfortunately, the buoy had shifted (something buoys sometimes do) about 400 feet from its proper position.

At approximately 1:30 a.m., the ship struck the reef. She was traveling at 12 knots, and the jolt was strong enough that the captain felt the vibration and rushed back to the bridge. He knew there was damage, but he didn't know how much. Wisely, he didn't wait to find out. He immediately directed all passengers to put on their life jackets and go to their muster stations.

Then he ordered the ship driven up onto a nearby sandbar.

"He did *what*?!" I said when I was told that the captain had given the order to ram the ship up onto a sandbar. I was already en route to our Incident Response Center and was being briefed on the incident. If I wasn't fully awake when I got the call at 2:00 a.m., I certainly was now.

As the surprise wore off, I realized his decision was both very clever and the ultimate validation of alignment. Without hesitation, he had acted to ensure the safety of our guests and crew in accordance with our culture's highest priority: safety. Beaching the ship damaged the hull, but it eliminated any risk to the guests and crew. Good for him. He acted promptly and deliberately.

As the response team assembled, our immediate challenge was how to help roughly 2,300 passengers who were about to be evacuated onto an island with no available hotel rooms. Someone grabbed the airline guide (this was long before online access to airlines) and began checking available flights. The next morning's flights had exactly eight available seats. Now, we only had to assist the remaining 2,292 people.

Alignment means acting decisively in accordance with your culture's highest priorities.

Through the night, our team scrambled to secure lodging and transportation options for every guest. We took over hotel ballrooms for temporary shelter. We chartered aircraft, routing passengers not just to Miami but to San Juan, where they could find hotel rooms. Who knew you could hire 737 and 747 aircraft at 3:00 in the morning?

The complexities kept multiplying. The passengers had evacuated without their belongings—no luggage, no passports, no clean underwear. The solution? Send two crew members into every cabin to pack their bags and retrieve them. But how to get the luggage back to its rightful owners? Many decisions had to be made in a short period of time, and it could have been paralyzing. How do we support our guests? How much do we spend to provide that support?

In a crisis, already having alignment on key principles is liberating. Just as the captain had prioritized the safety of the guests and crew over damage to our very expensive ship, our Miami team focused on the singular goal of making the guests as comfortable as possible and getting them home quickly. Our culture ensured that neither calculating the cost of the event nor trying to assign blame had any part in the evening's activities. That could wait for another day.

The team convinced Hertz and Avis to clear their entire rental-car lots, creating a giant baggage-claim area. Even that wasn't enough room, but it was a good start. We brought meals into the ballrooms and other shared spaces where the guests were taking shelter while they waited. Even our culinary group came to help and tried to make the meals as good as possible. We couldn't provide our usual WOW, but everyone worked hard to deliver an impressive response.

The ship's safes presented another challenge. To open them and remove guest valuables, we sent in security officers with camera crews and videotaped every safe opening. A large proportion of our guests had left their passports in those safes. We then had to deal with the twin challenges of either reuniting our guests with their documents or convincing US immigration authorities to let a few thousand people enter the US without IDs.

The ship also provided a central safe for passengers who preferred not to use the in-cabin safes. This full-wall unit needed to be removed intact. The team spent hours negotiating with customs to allow the entire unit to be transported, unopened, to the United States.

Tracking the dispersed passengers proved particularly difficult. The company's systems were binary, designed to tell us whether or not someone was on the ship. We hadn't planned for tracking thousands of people scattered across various hotels, ballrooms, and airport waiting areas. The team struggled to coordinate charter flights with displaced passengers, some of whom had wandered from their assigned waiting spots to find coffee or meals.

The dedication and problem-solving skills displayed by our employees got us through this crisis and brought all our guests home safely. Later, there would be time for reviewing the root causes of the accident and taking appropriate steps going forward. But now was a time to be thankful that what could have been a major incident turned out to be not much more than an interesting story for our guests to tell their children.

As a matter of interest, in the days after the incident, naval experts confirmed that there had been no need to beach the ship. Their tests showed that the ship was still stable even with the big gash in the side. She returned to the States on her own power. Redundancies built into the ship design (especially the double hull and watertight bulkheads) had kept her safe. Nevertheless, at the moment of crisis, the captain couldn't be sure of that, and he acted prudently and cautiously.

A team that is aligned and practices continuous improvement can respond to almost anything.

We learned many lessons that night and the next day, including strengthening navigation protocols, creating systems for tracking evacuated guests, and improving arrangements for feeding a tired incident response team. In the months ahead, we instituted more practice runs for emergency situations and focused on emergency communication.

NOROVIRUS

In 2024, I was given a tour of a new hospital in Miami. In the gleaming new operating room, I *ooh*ed and *aah*ed about the impressive equipment and the cleanliness of the space. But I couldn't resist pointing out that the OR would not pass muster as a galley on a cruise ship.

That is because sanitation rules on cruise ships are so stringent that no restaurant on land—and few hospitals—could meet them.

In this case, the difference in requirements was minor: The hospital had used pop rivets to mount the stainless-steel wall coverings. On a cruise ship, the rules require that the stainless steel be welded rather than riveted because the pop rivets have tiny holes where bacteria can accumulate.

Ironically, we in the cruise industry strongly support these strict requirements from the Centers for Disease Control and Prevention (CDC) because we believe that extreme safety standards protect the health of our guests and crew—and thereby protect our reputation. It is a bit like the safety standards that apply to airplanes; extreme safety measures make air travel a reliably safe mode of transportation, an essential factor for the airline industry's success.

Despite our over-the-top sanitary standards, the *Maritime Megaphone Multiplier* applies on steroids whenever there's a health issue at sea. The CDC estimates that there are 19 million to 21 million cases of norovirus in the United States every year, yet only a fraction of a percent happen on cruise ships—although you would never know it from the headlines.

I suppose I should feel flattered that our industry commands such attention. Some people even call norovirus the "cruise ship disease" despite more than 99 percent of cases occurring on land. A key reason is that cruise ship illnesses must be reported to the CDC, which publicly shares the data, while land-based outbreaks go unreported.

However, I will note two important points: First, despite exaggerations from some media of cruise ship illnesses, demand for cruising continues to grow. This demonstrates that the public is good at judging for themselves how minimal the safety risks are for cruises. And second, the statistics show that our crew members experience only a small fraction of the norovirus cases that our guests do. It always impresses me that, when we do have an outbreak on a ship, very few crew members get sick. It is not that our crew are superhuman (although sometimes I think they are). It's because they are very diligent about washing their hands! Are you?

OIL POLLUTION

Some "What the Hell?!" moments forced us to rethink our business model, while others challenged our self-perception and our faith in our culture. In 1994, the Coast Guard, using special radar equipment, spotted oil in the water behind one of our ships. They opened an investigation, and I asked our head of Marine Operations to conduct his own investigation. Unfortunately, he discovered that the findings were true.

Oil often leaks in an engine room, he explained, and it mixes with the water in the bilge, the lowest part of the ship. Our ships were equipped with purification equipment to separate the oil from the water, but the equipment was difficult to operate and worked poorly. His investigation determined that a number of our engineers on numerous ships deliberately discharged the oily water without first purifying it. Apparently, they viewed the rule around oily water as an unrealistic regulation that could be ignored.

I was aghast. More than 30 years later, I am still embarrassed by this sorry chapter in Royal's environmental history. We paid a hefty fine, but the real issue was how it could have happened in the first place and what we would do about it.

We took the obvious direct steps—adding more monitoring equipment to prevent tampering, upgrading systems, and increasing audit frequency. However, enforcement alone is a blunt tool. While a solid enforcement mechanism is necessary, true success comes from alignment. You can accomplish only so much by threats of punishment. But you can accomplish anything if your team is aligned and motivated. Purpose wins out over fear every time.

Purpose wins out over fear every time.

I knew that most of our mariners genuinely cared about the environment. Many cherished their time sailing or fishing or hiking or doing other nature-conscious activities. But enthusiasm for the environment is not the same as a commitment to protecting it. The number of engineers who violated these rules—or who knew of violations and stayed silent—made it clear that true alignment with Royal Caribbean's values was still missing.

When facing major challenges, the company has often looked beyond its ranks for exceptional expertise. For example, in 2001 when Enron's accounting scandal made us want to strengthen our accounting controls, we appointed the ex-CEO of Ernst & Young to lead our audit committee. During COVID, we turned to former leaders of the CDC and the Department of Health and Human Services (HHS). To drive alignment on environmental issues, we enlisted Bill Reilly, former head of the US Environmental Protection Agency (EPA) and the World Wildlife Fund (WWF).

Bringing in such distinguished leaders served two key purposes. First, they had the experience to deliver the results we needed. Second, their presence sent a powerful message about our priorities: We were committed enough to seek out the very best.

We turned to Bill Reilly to help us address this issue. With his encouragement, we adopted the ABC Program, which stood for *Above and Beyond Compliance*. We wanted to remind everyone that compliance with the rules was not the objective but the minimum.

We also created a new position: shipboard environmental officer. It was a significant step forward—but initially not as effective as we had hoped. I had assumed the ship's officers would collaborate to integrate environmental concerns into our priorities and procedures. Instead, the new environmental officers lacked a shared frame of reference with the rest of the crew, who saw them more as traffic cops handing out tickets than as partners in sustainability.

We quickly recognized the need to make this new role an integral step in an engineer's career path. Our goal was for these officers to incorporate an environmental perspective into the ship's operations, aligning with and supersizing our culture of breaking down silos and fostering cross-functional collaboration.

The result of the change was significant. Within 18 months, the environmental officers became more energized and better integrated. No longer seen as police, they were now accepted as partners. The program inspired our people, providing another source of pride and another reason to give their all to keep improving. That made us a stronger company.

People who look at such things tell me that they can feel the environmental commitment throughout the ship when they talk to our people, regardless of their position. While we still audit our performance, the true success of the program lies in the alignment of thousands of crew members, all unified by the shared value of caring for and protecting the environment.

HURRICANES

I'm often asked how much hurricanes impact our business, and people are surprised when I report that they are not normally a big concern. Hurricanes typically move at 10–15 mph, and our ships can travel over 20 mph, so with modern storm-modeling technology, it is relatively easy to navigate around a big storm. The main downside is having to reroute the ship to alternate destinations. This is a major logistical challenge for our team, but one they have learned to handle with aplomb. It is particularly inconvenient if the storm is due to be at a port on embarkation day. Fortunately, this is rare, and even then, our guests are usually understanding.

About 10 years ago, we decided to innovate in the area of weather prediction by adding a professional meteorologist to our staff instead of only seeking expert weather advice on an ad hoc basis. Every ship's captain views themselves as an expert about the weather, because seeking the calmest seas is an important part of their job. Nevertheless, as we expanded, hiring an expert with formal training and experience was a natural next step. Like so many continuous improvement initiatives, this one has proven even more beneficial than we expected. Our Meteorological Department not only helps our navigators plot their courses for the smoothest rides and lowest energy consumption but also provides localized color commentary on the weather, which our guests love.

SEPTEMBER 11, 2001

None of the challenges we encountered were dire enough to put our business at risk . . . until September 11, 2001. On that day, as we watched images of jet planes crashing into the Twin Towers, we knew that our world would never be the same, but we didn't know what changes would follow.

On balance, I personally believe our performance in handling the short-term issues after 9/11 was commendable. However, our handling of the longer-term consequences was, at best, adequate. And at Royal Caribbean, "adequate" is a failing grade.

> **Understanding both the short-term issues and the long-term consequences of a crisis is crucial.**

Understanding both aspects was crucial for continuous improvement and significantly shaped our response to subsequent crises.

In the first hours after the Twin Towers were destroyed, we just watched the news on television in shock. We activated our Incident Response Center, but we had no real response to make. Effectively, the Response Center became a sophisticated TV room with three big screens that played the same scenes over and over. There was no Department of Homeland Security back then and our normal sources of information—the FBI, Coast Guard, police, Secret Service, etc.—were as clueless as we were.

Soon, we recognized that immediate challenges demanded our attention. With 50,000 guests and 20,000 crew members aboard our ships, their families were desperate for reassurance that their loved ones were safe. There was no immediate panic, but you could feel it looming just beneath the surface. With all commercial flights grounded, there was growing anxiety about how guests would return home. Our call centers were overwhelmed, receiving over 300,000 calls that day—nearly six times our usual volume.

We had few answers to the legitimate questions being asked, and there was little we could do. The government had control, and all we could do was watch their actions with concern. The most critical challenge for us was communication—with guests on board, their families, future guests, business partners, and others. This was 2001, so satellite technology was still limited and unreliable. Despite these obstacles, I was deeply impressed by how quickly our Incident

Response teams mobilized. They extended hours for call center staff, brought in additional support from other departments, and even arranged for masseuses to help relieve some of the stress on our overworked team.

Even with the limited satellite capacity of the early 2000s, all our guests and crew were able to talk to their loved ones relatively quickly. We used more satellite bandwidth that week than in the rest of the year combined. (Of course, what seemed like massive satellite traffic that day was slightly less than an average day today.)

A critical unknown was when airplanes would be allowed to fly, so we had to continuously revise our contingency plans. Fortunately, the spirit of our guests was remarkably understanding. They recognized that we were in uncharted waters (pun intended) and accepted that our uncertain and changing answers were the best that could be expected under the circumstances.

Ramping up security was another need. Several years earlier, we had prepared for bomb threats being made against individual ships. As a precaution, we had positioned screening equipment (magnetometers and X-ray equipment) in our embarkation ports. Originally, the equipment was intended to only address isolated threats to individual ships, but now we needed to adapt it to screen every vessel.

Our security teams did a terrific job activating all this equipment around the world on short notice. As a result, by the weekend after the attack, we were prepared to screen every person and every bit of material entering our ships. It was slow at first, because we had a limited number of machines, but it worked. Within a few weeks, we were at full speed. By comparison, it took the airlines over a year to reach the same standard.

It is also noteworthy that we did not act alone. We are an intensely competitive industry and spend most of our time thinking of how to outmaneuver the other guy. Except on safety. On issues of safety, all the cruise lines worked cooperatively, not competitively.

Of course, we made mistakes. I laughed when I was told that we were confiscating fingernail clippers at embarkation, but if you ordered room service, we would deliver steak knives to your stateroom.

In the absence of solid information, we were open and candid about sharing what information we did have and tried to address our guests' concerns. On the ships, we asked the captains to have their officers spend most of their time walking around the public areas. Many officers have jobs that take place out of sight—on the bridge, in the engine control room, doing paperwork, etc. We asked them to put any nonessential duties aside and remain visible. It is remarkable how calming it is to see officers in crisp white uniforms simply talking with the guests about the situation. In times of crisis, people want to connect with others.

In times of crisis, people want to connect with others.

A "NEW NORMAL"?

In the aftermath of 9/11, the phrase *new normal* suddenly gained traction. While the term wasn't new, it quickly became a popular shorthand for the deep societal shifts many observers considered inevitable.

In our office and within the investment community, there were many who believed air travel would never recover. This school of thought believed that travelers were paralyzed by fear, and that no amount of security measures or price cuts would be capable of alleviating that deep, visceral anxiety. They were sure that our revenues were about to plummet, and the prevailing sentiment was that our business model as a travel company was doomed.

Given this view of the world, the new-normal mindset insisted that Royal Caribbean's only option was to slash costs—food, advertising, research and development, and investment in new ships. We should abandon our strategy of differentiating the company through innovation and quality. To survive, we would have to forsake our North Star.

It was an existential threat to our business, our growth trajectory, and the culture we had worked so hard to build.

If it was true.

Despite the widespread sense of doom and gloom, I saw reason for optimism. In the week following 9/11, our bookings dropped by 50 percent—a staggering decline, the worst in our history. Was this proof that our business was doomed? It seemed like the end was near.

Cue scenes of panic.

But then I thought—wasn't it more shocking that we received any bookings at all? After all, these people had just witnessed this horrific attack on American soil and still decided to plan their spring vacation. What was remarkable wasn't that our bookings had fallen by half. What was truly remarkable was that, even in those first few chaotic days after the attack, thousands of people still chose to book their vacations.

It was a tough time, yes.

But a new normal? Not so much.

Just as we had learned in 1987 after the Black Monday stock market crash, people were far more resilient than the media gave them credit for. One example still gives me goosebumps. That first week, a family of five from Seattle called our reservation desk about their cruise scheduled for Sunday. Our representative explained that since no planes were flying, we'd refund their money and offer a coupon for their next cruise. But the family refused.

"No terrorist is going to ruin our vacation," the mother said. "If planes aren't flying, we will simply drive to the port." "Simply" drive 3,000 miles to the port? Sometimes it's our guests who deliver the WOW. I remember thinking that by the end of their journey, either they'd be a stronger family or they would never speak to each other again.

The nation was consumed by fear, and I fielded calls every day from investors who urged drastic action to bring our stock price up. Every caller was insistent that they wanted to focus on the long term, but underlying every call was a demand that we announce a major cost-cutting program to bring the share price up now.

The message was clear: Pay lip service to the long term but only pay attention to next week.

PRITZKER'S SURPRISING CALL

Then, in the middle of the second week after 9/11, just as I was struggling with all the pressure to focus on the near-term, I got a call from Tom Pritzker, one of our biggest shareholders and longest-serving board members. Tom was a good friend who always had good insights about world events and I was eager to hear his take on the current unprecedented situation.

"Richard, I know you're getting pressure for quick results," he said. "I know it seems like you have to take strong immediate action. I just want to remind you that we're not interested in selling anytime soon. And neither are most of your shareholders. Your focus should be on where the company needs to be three years from now, or five, or seven. Not next month and not next year. I don't know what that means in terms of the actions that you take, but that should be your guiding principle."

Even in that period of intense crisis and widespread doubt about the industry, he was reminding me about the importance of our North Star and our long-term focus. Having a friend and director of Tom's stature providing such encouragement and sage counsel was breathtaking and highly reassuring.

His advice and his support had a dual impact. It helped calm my fears—it reminded me that I wasn't alone in fighting short-term pressures—but it also invigorated me to focus on the longer term.

We started a program called Survive and Thrive. It had two goals: minimize our losses in the short term but prepare ourselves to thrive when the crisis passed. With Tom's words uppermost in my mind, I tried to project a sense of calm and confidence.

One of the most enduring and helpful lessons from this history was a greater appreciation of the importance of visibility. I am by nature a private person and far prefer to work in a small group environment than in the public eye. But it quickly became clear that people needed to know that the company was going to overcome these challenges and emerge strong. And, whether I liked it or not, an important part of my job and the job of our other leaders was to personify that confidence.

Across the leadership team, we all spent extra time meeting with people throughout the organization, reinforcing the message that our long-term vision had not changed. Simply being seen and demonstrating confidence was crucial.

Unfortunately, no matter what we said, the daily barrage of negative imagery was overwhelming. We all spoke the same words—"We will survive, and we will thrive"—but too many people acted as if the real message was, "Do whatever it takes to survive. And maybe try to thrive a little." The consequence was predictable: failing alignment.

We didn't excel at either cutting costs or preparing for the future. Individual decision-makers throughout the organization made well-intentioned but suboptimal choices for the thousands of decisions that needed to be made every day. We served cheaper cuts of beef, bought less advertising, and killed exciting capital projects. Some of the cost-saving measures were necessary, but the inconsistency and short-term focus meant that the decisions were not well-balanced. Too often, we traded small immediate benefits for a longer-term risk to the WOW. In this instance, I tried to keep everyone focused on the long-term future, but I was too tentative and didn't do enough to overcome the intensity of voices predicting doom.

Fortunately, the recovery from 9/11 was relatively quick, and the long-term impact on our bookings and our business was far less than so many feared. We ended up with yields (the revenue a ship makes per berth) down only 10 percent compared to the prior year. Painful, yes—even very painful—but not catastrophic. If this traumatic, world-changing event meant that people were still willing to pay us 90 percent of what they had paid the year before, then it was not the end of the

Explicit and more extensive communications become even more impactful during a crisis.

world as we knew it. Within a year, bookings were already bouncing back to the level of our previous highs.

We had thrived despite our imperfect response to the crisis. But we did learn from the experience. I resolved that in the future, we would be more careful to emphasize the long-term strategy in our communications and have more extensive discussions about our choices so that everyone understood and remained aligned on our strategy.

Those lessons and our commitment to continuous improvement served us well during subsequent and even more existential crises such as the COVID-19 pandemic.

MEDICAL CARE

Although medical issues don't fall into the category of disasters in the traditional sense, they are still a vital concern for us and our guests and our crew. We need to apply the same level of focus and care to this area that we dedicate to other important matters.

The human body is extraordinary. It is so complex, so resilient, so functional that I can't think about it without a sense of wonder. How is it possible that all these intricate systems work together so fluidly without constantly breaking down? We can't make a coffee machine that doesn't need constant maintenance, but if I cut myself while chopping carrots, my body will quickly repair itself—no manual required.

Of course, even this marvel of nature needs help occasionally. On our ships, we are conscious of the awesome responsibility to not only keep eight million guests a year happy and entertained but also to deal with injuries or illness when they happen. That is where our medical centers come in. And here, the lessons of continuous improvement are particularly relevant, because medical science is advancing at such an astonishing pace.

The most notable change we've embraced over the last few years has been the availability of specialist advice. Medical science has improved by leaps and bounds, but no doctor can possibly know everything about every condition. In addition, I remember my father's adage that "Two heads are better than one, even if one is a dunderhead." That's why we have established partnerships with several leading medical centers, including the Cleveland Clinic and the University of Miami Health System, to provide telemedicine assistance. In keeping with our practice of bringing in top-level experts in specialized areas, we brought in the secretary of health for the State of Pennsylvania as our chief medical officer.

I recall one evening when I got a panicky call from my brother-in-law. He was on a cruise (smart guy) with my two nieces when their roughhousing got out of hand and one of them hurt her hand in a door jamb. My brother-in-law wanted to know how good our doctors were because he was unsure about the treatment. I asked our chief medical officer, who, in turn, called a leading hand specialist at the Mayo Clinic. That doctor laughed and said, "I trained him, and he's excellent." He went on to say that the treatment plan was exactly what he would have done. Her hand healed completely, and today, she is an expert violinist. (Actually not, but her hand is fine.)

BODY CAMS

People often ask why our security folks all wear body cams. It all started with a single incident that happened to be caught on a guest's video. One day, a guest was angry and unruly (yes, that happens). Two security guards were called to deal with the problem, and the guest started yelling at the guards in a highly provocative manner (yes, that happens too).

What impressed me was how well the guards responded. They were cool, professional, and generally worked to deescalate the encounter.

Hands at their sides, expressions neutral, voices calm, they were awesome, textbook perfect.

It occurred to me that it was only luck that we had a video of the encounter. Wouldn't it be helpful if we got body cams for all our security team? When I went to our head of security with this highly original idea, she laughed and pulled three brochures out of her drawer. She was several steps ahead of me and had been researching cameras for months.

It turns out that while the idea is simple, the mechanics are complicated, ranging from how to attach it to a person's body to how to store the vast amounts of footage. Once we adopted it fleet-wide, it proved its worth, but not in the way we expected. We thought it would provide proof of what happened in any given encounter. It did that, but the real benefit was that it made every encounter calmer. We learned that whenever there was a confrontation, the guard would say something like "Just so you know, we're recording this discussion." Immediately, the temperature would drop by five degrees, and you could feel the tension ease. The guest would become more measured, and I'm sure that the camera made the guard more careful. It effortlessly defused potential conflicts.

I know that body cams aren't perfect, but they are undoubtedly effective.

DEEPER LESSON

The deeper lesson in all these situations is the importance of staying true to your culture, even when your company is severely stressed. Yes, these events will happen, unpredictably and relentlessly. Yes, they can be frightening and frustrating. Through every "What the Hell?!" moment—from groundings to germs to oil spills and hurricanes—the lesson is always the same: Culture matters. Alignment matters.

KEY TAKEAWAYS

- In moments of crisis, alignment around core values (like safety) enables decisive action.
- Conventional solutions often fail; reframing the problem unlocks innovation.
- Rules alone don't drive behavior; embedding values into culture does.

Know the ropes:

Old sailing ships were marvels of engineering with intricate systems of masts and sails that were controlled by a complicated series of ropes. New recruits on a ship had to learn each rope by name and function. Today, the metaphor still holds. The best leaders are those who've made the effort to *learn the ropes*.

7

Innovation in Ship Design

The success of *Sovereign of the Seas*—and our other earlier ships—had surpassed even our most ambitious expectations. But it wasn't enough.

Our North Star has always been twofold: to become a preeminent force in the broader vacation market, and to deliver the best vacation anywhere, driven by exceptional service, innovation, and quality.

Innovation in ship design was essential to that vision. The best way to understand how that innovation came to life is through the ships themselves—and the purposeful decisions that shaped them.

PREEMPTIVE PRESS RELEASES

A happy accident resulted in a practice that has proven to be exceptionally impactful as a driver of innovative design.

We were reviewing early concepts for a new ship. The team's proposals were nice but uninspiring. We wanted groundbreaking, and they were offering novel. We wanted spectacular, and they were proposing beautiful.

It was so frustrating. We kept saying, "These designs are good, but we need something better," and they kept replying: "If these concepts are so good, why aren't you happy?" We tried to explain that we wanted to offer our guests not just better but truly exceptional—transformational, not just enhanced.

Then we put it a different way. We asked the team to imagine themselves a month before delivery of the ship, drafting the press release that would describe what made the new ship so special. "How would you describe it in a press release? What would you hope people would say about it to their neighbors when they got home?" we asked.

When the designers tried to describe their designs as transformational in the release, the words wouldn't flow. They fell flat. Their written descriptions sounded nice but not inspired. The best way to clarify an idea in your own mind is to explain it to someone else. If the idea doesn't sound compelling on paper, it likely isn't.

The best way to clarify an idea in your own mind is to explain it to someone else.

The exercise had an immediate impact. At our next meeting, the designers took a completely different approach to the design, and we all applauded. The design was terrific—clearly transformational—and the explanation in the new draft release came across that way.

We were so impressed with the results of using the press release as a design tool rather than a marketing tactic that we continue to use it for most of our major projects. The ultimate press release (written three or four years later) was inevitably different from the draft used in the steering committee, but our early versions helped drive innovation.

TRANSFORM BUT STAY RELEVANT

Now we faced another potential problem of our own making. We had developed such a reputation for innovation that everyone wanted their area to be transformational. But even in the context of a transformational ship, our guests want a balance between things they are familiar with and things they never imagined.

The issue reminds me of a famous scene from *Back to the Future*, where Marty, having traveled back to the 1950s, performs Chuck Berry's "Johnny B. Goode" at a high school prom. Although the audience has never heard it before, they instantly connect with the sound and start dancing (it is a great song). Then Marty gets carried away and starts playing in a futuristic style with a screeching guitar solo. This new sound is a step too far for his audience, and they stop dancing and stare. Eventually, Marty realizes his mistake and quips, "I guess you guys aren't ready for that yet."

In designing our ships, we too needed balance. We needed to impress our audience with exciting new features but not turn them off by going too far from their comfort zone. Our first priority is to give our guests the amazing cruise that they already know and love. After we have done that, we can look to add new features that will take their enjoyment to another level.

To ensure that we maintained a good balance, we adopted a *rule of thirds*. The rule of thirds calls for new projects to be one-third traditional, one-third evolutionary, and one-third revolutionary. This framework gave us a common language for discussion and decision-making. It forced us to look at a ship as a holistic whole rather than a series of unrelated parts. It ensured that we stayed rooted in what our guests valued while also pushing the boundaries of what could be enhanced.

The rule of thirds helped us more than we expected. It disciplined every discussion. At project meetings, we would look at the various areas on board and list them by category. The person responsible for each area had to clearly articulate why that area fit into one category or the other and why that was appropriate. Statements like "This is beautiful" aren't responsive to the question of whether a proposal is traditional, evolutionary, or revolutionary.

WHAT'S IN A NAME?

Beyond frameworks, we also found that the energy around a project could be influenced by something as simple as its name. In the mid-1990s, when we were working on the design for *Voyager of the Seas*, I was concerned that the project was languishing. There was progress but it was very slow, and the project was not receiving the attention it deserved.

One Monday morning, I told our executive committee that I thought a project name would add impetus to the effort. We should give the project a name that would convey that we were planning the biggest cruise ship ever built. And I had the perfect name—Project Archimedes. Archimedes was famous for saying, "Give me a lever long enough and a fulcrum on which to place it, and I shall move the world." I thought Project Archimedes would be a clever choice for this project, since it would remind us daily that we were building something meant to move the world.

Rod McCleod, head of marketing and a great communicator, thought about it for perhaps 10 seconds and said, "That's a terrible name. It's too hard to understand, and besides, no one can spell it. The name should be something short and uplifting, like Project Eagle." And just like that, Project Eagle was born. Rod's proposed name took off and did all he hoped it would. It was uplifting and generated excitement. The people working on the project designated themselves Eagles; they named a conference room the Eagles Conference Room; we even had Entertainment Eagles and Dining Eagles.

In 2004, we launched Project Genesis, which became *Oasis of the*

Seas, one of the most successful designs in cruise ship history. The name reflected that we wanted to start with a clean sheet of paper and design something new and special. Similarly, when we embarked on building a new Celebrity ship in 2010, we named it Project Edge because we wanted to take the Celebrity design to the edge of what was possible. We also started Project Nova for Silversea reflecting a determination to create something truly novel, and it became the very successful *Silver Nova*.

In 2016, we decided that the time was right to build something totally new for the Royal Caribbean brand, and we thought we had an opportunity to create something special. We spent some time discussing the project name (much more than Rod's 10-second creation of Project Eagle) and quickly focused on Project Icon as an aspirational name. Aspirational because to be iconic, something needs to be timeless, recognizable, and influential. We knew that if we used that name, we would have to be unrelenting in executing a transformational design. But we also knew that the name would help give meaning to our ambitions and help everyone rally around the goal. It worked. The name Project Icon helped frame every discussion and I believe helped galvanize a determination to create something that lived up to its name . . . something iconic.

We don't yet have a Project Archimedes, but I haven't abandoned the idea. Maybe I'll talk to Jason Liberty about it.

CREATING THE ROYAL PROMENADE

From the earliest days—going all the way back to *Sovereign of the Seas*—we've been obsessed with one thing: making our ships feel intuitive. Guests shouldn't have to think about where they're going; the space should carry them.

The Centrum on *Sovereign* was a major breakthrough, and its successors only expanded on this vision, becoming even grander and more impressive. But as we entered the twenty-first century, we knew it was time to take these ideas to an entirely new level.

We wanted ships that would provide amenities and activities competitive with land-based vacations. However, the more places to go and the more alternatives you can choose from, the more confusing it can be to find your way there. Complexity was our enemy.

To overcome this, we needed some new approaches to ship design.

Normally, different spaces on the ship are arranged based on ease of construction, but we took a cue from our favorite cities and arranged our spaces like neighborhoods—clusters of activity with a distinct feel and function.

For example, if you stood outside the main theater on *Oasis*, you were surrounded by other entertainment venues, including Studio B (ice skating), a karaoke lounge (bad singing), a comedy club (bad jokes), a jazz club (cool jazz), a casino (good luck), and Boleros (Latin dancing). Each space has its own personality, but they belong together . . . in a neighborhood.

Neighborhooding like this was somewhat more expensive to build but substantially more convenient and intuitive for our guests. We decided that the extra effort and cost that this approach required would more than pay for itself in guest satisfaction.

However, before we could build those neighborhoods, we had to solve another problem. All these new options for our guests could not fit in *Sovereign*'s vertical atrium. The team decided that we needed an atrium (to be called the Royal Promenade) bigger than the one on *Sovereign*—as long as a football field.

It was a great idea, but the engineers said, "Not so fast."

The first challenge was structural. The engineers still thought of our atria as enormous holes in the middle of the ship that compromised structural integrity. Fortunately, we had Harri Kulovaara to oversee all our ship construction. Harri, a brilliant naval architect with a remarkable can-do attitude, brought a wealth of knowledge and experience to the table.

Having previously designed a ship with a horizontal atrium, Harri applied the same concept that made *Sovereign* possible. He worked closely with the structural engineers to ensure the atrium's integrity, essentially encasing it in a hard shell, like the exoskeleton on a beetle.*

For *Oasis*, our ambitions hit another roadblock when we reviewed fire bulkheads and doors. Fire safety requirements are, appropriately, very strict on cruise ships. Fireproof dividers are required at regular intervals. They are called A60 bulkheads: A to indicate that they are made of steel and block fire and 60 to indicate that they also block heat for up to 60 minutes.

Unfortunately, the largest A60 fire doors in existence at the time were only about 16 feet wide and 6 feet tall. For the very wide promenade we wanted on *Oasis*, we needed a door about 60 feet wide and 22 feet tall. That required either a dozen of the largest A60 doors or some new, very imaginative solution.

Fortunately, Harri, with the Finnish shipyard and his team, developed the idea of using two steel roll-up doors (like garage doors) made of steel slats. The doors operate in parallel and come down from the ceiling in pairs. The steel of the doors blocks fire, and the gap between the two doors prevents the transfer of heat. We have these doors now in all our new Royal Promenades, but unless they are lowered to the down position, you would never know they were there. It's my hope that nobody will ever need to see them except during drills.

COMPRESSION, THEN WONDER. MY FAVORITE SPOT

There's a spot I return to every time I'm on one of the newer Royal Caribbean ships. It's not on any deck plan, but I've come to think of

---

* Humans have endoskeletons, with the structure composed of strong bones inside our bodies and soft tissue on the outside. Beetles have exoskeletons, where all the structure is on the outside and the center is soft.

it as my personal checkpoint—a place where all the work behind the scenes comes into focus.

The spot is just inside the ship, where the embarkation corridor gives way to the Royal Promenade. Guests step from a low-ceilinged walkway into a soaring, unexpected space. It's a design principle that Frank Lloyd Wright was famous for. It is called *compression and expansion*, and Wright used it to create a sense of movement, a technique that makes a space feel more alive.

I like to stand there quietly and watch the reactions of our guests as they enter. Everyone pauses. Everyone looks up. Seasoned cruisers smile in recognition. First-timers literally gasp. They turn to each other and say, "The pictures don't do it justice."

It never gets old.

I like this spot because it validates so much of what we have worked so hard to accomplish. Surveys tell us a lot, but surveys don't convey the emotional weight that these involuntary reactions carry. After all the reviews, the revisions, the late-night debates—this is the moment that matters.

STUDIO B/ABSOLUTE ZERO

Our determination to expand the entertainment options on this new class of ships led to one of the more interesting technical challenges. Our ships already had several entertainment spaces, but we wanted to add one additional space that would be different from anything else on the high seas. Peter Compton, who led our entertainment team, proposed adding a flexible space that would be patterned after the second stage in a TV studio. He proposed calling it Studio B. Like a TV studio, there would be seating for the studio audience, and the space itself would be flexible enough to accommodate many kinds of activities.

It sounded great, but we had trouble understanding what entertainment or activities they had in mind. Dancers? Game shows? Sumo wrestlers? What? Peter kept saying that it could be "anything we wanted," but what we wanted was specifics.

Late one afternoon, Peter and some of his entertainment team arrived in my office wearing clown costumes and carrying popcorn. They took me to a nearby building where they had built staging on the scale of the proposed Studio B.

We spent two hours watching various performers, including singers and dancers. They even laid down a large piece of artificial ice (essentially a pad of Teflon) for a professional figure skater. It was all great fun, but the next act, a high school rollerblading club, was the surprise hit of the day. They danced, they jumped, and they spun around. They blew us away and won our hearts. The unexpected combination of rollerbladers and ice skating seemed like a winner.

In two hours, we went from fear that Studio B would be a problem to absolute confidence that it would be a great success. We knew we wanted an ice rink, but the skater said, "Skating on artificial ice is difficult. I can skate on it, but it lacks the gracefulness of real ice." We decided that we should proceed with Studio B but that the ice needed to be real, not artificial.

Naively, I thought that once we made the decision, the rest would be simple. Maybe we could order a skating rink off Amazon? We learned instead that normal ice-skating rinks are made by pouring concrete over refrigerant pipes. That works fine on land, but ships flex as they move through the water. Ice can bend (who knew?), but concrete breaks.

Harri spent a month studying the problem and returned with a solution. Instead of concrete, they designed a viscous layer, almost like mud, that stayed soft near the bottom but firmed up toward the top. It would bend, and our ice-skating rink would work.

Harri and I saw the rink at the Finnish shipyard just as they were finishing it. We watched as they flooded it with water and created a smooth sheet of ice. It looked incredible. We high-fived as the Zamboni started smoothing the surface. I had been nervous, but now I could see for myself that it worked. Success.

A Zamboni operator smooths the ice in Absolute Zero on *Icon of the Seas*.

Oops, we started celebrating a bit too early.

At dinner that evening, someone came to our table with an update. Although the ice looked good to us, the professional skater we had hired to test it reported that it was too warm and soft to skate on.

Really? Too warm?

My heart sank as I imagined our magnificent new ship, destined to sail with an empty Studio B at its core, simply because ice comes in varying degrees of coldness and hardness. Fortunately, Harri found a simple fix—a new refrigerant with a lower freezing point. It made the ice harder and colder and the skaters much happier.

The ice-skating rink was so successful that we have put it on 16 ships and become the largest employer of figure skaters in America. My heart leaps every time I watch a performance in Studio B and see those extraordinary skaters glide across the ice seemingly without effort, as if the laws of friction don't exist.

Adding an ice-skating rink on a ship turned out to be a difficult and expensive proposition. Yet it was our approach that made it a defining moment for our corporate culture. Our willingness to make such a major commitment spoke volumes about our unwavering dedication to our North Star.

> **People pay more attention to what we do than what we say.**

Ovation of the Seas "floated out" at the Meyer Werft shipyard in Papenburg, Germany.

The first atrium at sea—the Centrum on *Monarch of the Seas*.

Ed Stephan, the founder of Royal Caribbean.

Oasis of the Seas on sea trial off the coast of Sweden, towing the experimental blimp.

The experimental blimp in the factory. Note the workers near the rear fin for scale.

Installing the AquaDome roof on *Icon of the Seas*.

Azipods propel the ship and
increase maneuverability.

A Zamboni operator smoothing the ice in
Absolute Zero on *Icon of the Seas*.

The Magic Carpet on *Celebrity Edge*.

Perfect Day at CocoCay.

CAVE Renderings

As part of the design process for a new ship, the company makes renderings of various spaces. Here are two examples of renderings made during the design process for *Icon of the Seas* alongside photos taken at delivery several years later. Not all renderings are this accurate, but they are all helpful in designing the ship.

Overlooking Central Park on *Icon of the Seas*.

The Pearl on *Icon of the Seas*.

Richard pouring martinis in the Martini Bar on *Celebrity Edge*.

The Pearl under construction at the shipyard in Finland.

The author at the shipyard, driving an early version of bumper cars for use on *Quantum*-class ships.

Richard trying out the Flowrider surf simulator on board *Oasis of the Seas*.

The author diving in the Philippines while announcing a new environmental initiative.

Getting a feel for the sky diving simulator onboard *Quantum of the Seas*.

A cold swim for Richard, trying out a Survival Suit in frigid Alaskan waters.

The author testing his lungs with a troupe of bagpipers ahead of a naming ceremony.

Crew appreciation dinners

Taking dinner orders.

The author, serving dinner.

The entire temporary "wait staff" gathers before dinner.
Everyone was too tired to do an after-dinner picture.

Crew

It isn't all work! At a party for *Navigator of the Seas* crew.

WOWing one of our younger guests in Adventure Ocean.

A chef adds a sprig of parsley to a salmon filet.

A crew member congratulates a young guest for her Flowrider skills.

A crew member reviews the schedule with a guest.

Crew

Pruning plants on *Harmony of the Seas*.

Pouring drinks with gusto.

A cabana attendant delivers drinks to a thirsty cabana crowd.

Maintenance continues around the clock. A cleaner vacuums the stairs at night on *Ovation of the Seas*.

In the CAVE, staff and crew look at virtual reality images of the AquaDome on *Icon of the Seas*.

Symphony of the Seas arrives at the state-of-the-art Terminal A in Miami.

The message "make it real, or don't do it" carried far more weight than countless corporate memos on strategy.

In the end, people pay more attention to what we do than what we say.

Looking back, the ice rink confirmed something important: Stay true to your North Star and do it right. That commitment to excellence and intentionality—exemplified by the ice rink—became a fabled story at Royal Caribbean and continues to inspire our culture to go to extremes to WOW our guests.

THE CAVE

In 2015, Harri Kulovaara and I visited a design office of Chantiers de l'Atlantique, in St Nazaire, France, where we saw a small virtual reality (VR) simulator. We were there to review the design of *Celebrity Edge* and the construction progress of *Harmony of the Seas*. The simulator was impressive, and we were amazed at how helpful it was to visualize the spaces on board and to imagine how they would feel to a guest.

On the flight home, Harri and I talked at length about how such technology could enhance our design process. When we got home, we talked more about the idea and about expanding the concept to encompass a full high-tech design center in Miami. We asked Kelly Gonzalez to design an extension to our office to accommodate all the technology needed to make this an effective facility. Kelly oversees all interior design across Royal Caribbean Group ships and has a rare talent for bringing out the best in the hundreds of architects and designers involved. Her superpower is a unique blend of artistic vision and practical application. It enables her to shape vastly different experiences–from the 7,600-guest *Icon of the Seas* to the intimate 100-guest *Celebrity Flora*.

Kelly designed a 20,000 square-foot facility that included large and small collaboration spaces, support spaces, and enormous computer screens (up to 32 feet wide). The centerpiece of the design was a large VR room—called a CAVE, for *computer aided virtual environment*. The idea was to create a state-of-the-art Innovation Lab, where architects, designers, operations experts, and executives could come together and collaborate on new and better experiences for our guests.

As with any major investment at Royal Caribbean, the project required a formal CAR (a Capital Appropriations Request, designed to ensure that all capital expenditures are properly reviewed and approved). Soon after the CAR was submitted, the CAR committee chair came to see Jason and me.

She wanted to talk to us about the CAR for the Innovation Lab. "This is a little embarrassing," she said, "but the committee has unanimously concluded that the project does not have an adequate payback to justify giving our approval." At that point, she paused and added, "We know that you'll probably overrule us, but you've always told us to give you our best advice, and that is what we are doing."

The CAVE wasn't necessary to build a *great* ship, but it was critical to build an *exceptional* one.

Jason and I laughed. "You are right on both points," I said. "We *will* overrule you because we are convinced of its value. But," I went on, "you are also right that you should give us your best advice, and we appreciate that you have done precisely that. That's the best news we've had all day."

We went ahead and built the Innovation Lab, and it's been a transformational success. The head of operations for the shipyard in Turku, Finland, said it best: "We used to take months of meetings and drawings to align on a design. Now we put on goggles, walk through the ship together, and settle it all in 30 minutes. It's like speaking a new language."

The early projects we used the CAVE for were *Celebrity Edge, Icon of the Seas*, and Perfect Day. In each case, the CAVE dramatically reduced the design time, but I got a sense of another key value when our head of Dining Services spoke to me about his experience. He told me that he had just reviewed the design of one of the main dining spaces on board *Edge* using the CAVE. He was awestruck.

"On previous ships," he said, "The plans and renderings of the dining rooms always looked fine. But using the CAVE, I could see problems with the design I would never have seen otherwise. For example, the path a waiter would take to deliver food was awkward. To make sure the food is delivered hot, the waiter needs a clear pathway, and with the CAVE, I could see that the pathways were difficult. A few simple tweaks fixed it, but, prior to the CAVE, I never would have seen the problem until the ship was built."

I call this advantage *democratizing the process*. Previously, only a small group of people could impact the design because few people are comfortable reading architect drawings. This CAVE technology allows anyone—even with no architectural experience—to see, understand, and meaningfully contribute. That makes for better collaboration and innovation.

The CAVE is a good example of the importance of commitment to a goal. The CAVE wasn't *necessary* to build a great ship, but it was critical to build an *exceptional* one. It is also a good example of continuous improvement being instilled in the organization because today—10 years later—the company is already finalizing work on its replacement (a proprietary system using goggles that provide even greater flexibility and realism).

THE ROCK WALL

In 1998, while finalizing the design for *Voyager of the Seas*, we noticed a large, empty space behind the funnel. I asked three members of the Eagles team to imagine something interesting to put there. These were younger members of the group who were so new to the team that they called themselves *Eaglets*.

I thought that they would appreciate the challenge and might approach it from a different perspective. They studied it for several weeks and returned with a proposal for a rock-climbing wall. The vertical space was perfect, they explained, and there was plenty of space for equipment. They pointed out that rock climbing was one of the fastest-growing sports in America and especially popular with our younger guests.

I resisted. I could not imagine anyone wanting to change into special gear on vacation and climb a wall. I didn't tell them, but I privately went to a climbing studio and tried it myself. I came away with several bruises and a conviction that no reasonable person would find this fun. I asked them to come back with three "more reasonable" alternatives.

The Eaglets came back saying, "As you requested, we have developed three alternative ideas. But we looked further into the rock climbing and are convinced that it would be a winner." They insisted on presenting all four ideas, again including the rock wall. I hated all four ideas, but I thought the rock wall was the least terrible, so I agreed to it.

When the finished ship arrived in Miami, everyone started talking about the rock wall. The cruise director commented, "Only a fraction of guests actually climb the wall, but it's one of the most photographed features on board. It tells everyone this ship is different." It was so popular that we retrofitted it on our existing ships and have since included it on every new ship.

Now, I like to joke that it was one of my best ideas.

The success of the wall surprised me, but we gained three useful insights.

First, it reminded us that not everything we offered had to appeal to everyone. The dynamic was similar to the Champagne Bar on *Sovereign*. Not all guests wanted to sip champagne in a specialized bar, but the presence of the opportunity spoke to many people. Similarly, although only 10 percent of our guests use the rock-climbing wall, its presence speaks volumes about the cruise experience.

Second, it became highly symbolic of the shift we were trying to make in people's perception of cruising. It is hard to think of cruising as a sedentary vacation when it offers things like rock climbing, ice skating, sky diving, waterslides, and surfing.

The third and most important learning was that inspiration is everywhere. If we give our people the opportunity to be creative, they will be. They are passionate, diligent, and persistent. They don't just deliver the WOW, they are the WOW.

THE BLIMP, THE STORM, AND THE SWEDISH AIR FORCE

Not all our ideas were successful. Some of them were spectacular failures. And when we fail, we do so with panache.

One such spectacular failure was the idea of putting a blimp on *Oasis of the Seas.*

The idea was to add a blimp that could be towed 500 feet in the air above the ship to give our guests a view of the ship and its surroundings. Besides being an exciting guest experience, it would be a distinctive feature visible to people miles away.

The concept was technically very challenging; it had to be able to withstand hurricane force winds and still be comfortable for 12 guests at a time. And it had to be tested under the most difficult of conditions—first in computer simulations, then in a wind tunnel, then on a special racing track, and finally on board the ship during sea trials off the coast of Sweden.

I had to try it. The safety officer on board agreed but only if she came with me and we both wore life jackets. I was not sure what a life jacket would do for me hundreds of feet in the air, but that was the requirement, so I put on my vest, ignored my fear of heights, and up we went.

The view of the coast of Sweden was extraordinary. Miles of coastline and open water stretched in every direction. As we ascended, the world below seemed to grow smaller, and the panorama that unfolded before us was breathtaking. But as the blimp got to 400 feet, my acrophobia became impossible to ignore, and the safety officer calmly guided us back down. Once back on solid ground (i.e., the ship's deck), the safety officer who had been quiet during the ride—couldn't stop talking about the view, how awe-inspiring it had been, and how blown away our guests would be.

The proper cradle for the blimp wasn't ready, so the crew tied the blimp down to temporary moorings, and we all went to sleep. That night, there was a storm. While I was cozy in my cabin, the blimp broke free of its temporary moorings and flew away. Before we could find it, the captain received a call from the Swedish Air Force. Apparently, our blimp had floated into commercial air space, and the Air Force wanted to shoot it down. Luckily, before they opened fire, the blimp started descending and fell into the ocean. A fishing boat eventually picked it up.

We decided that the blimp was not meant to be! We concluded that the ship had so many other special features that adding a blimp would be gilding the lily. But the blimp idea still made its point: We were determined to make *Oasis* another transformational advance in ship design, and we were willing to go to exceptional lengths (and heights) to advance toward that North Star. And just as importantly, we were willing to let go when an idea didn't fit.

Oasis of the Seas **during sea trials with the experimental blimp off the cost of Sweden.**

CELEBRITY EDGE **AND THE MAGIC CARPET**

The Royal Caribbean brand established its shipbuilding reputation with increasingly larger ships, newer features, and conversation-starting activities. Now, as we developed ships for the sister brand, Celebrity, we wanted to offer smaller ships that visited more unusual locations. The style would emphasize elegance and fine food over thrills.

Did our design team have the flexibility to design a smaller but still amazing ship for this very different guest experience?

We started with a steering committee as we had done since the design of *Sovereign*. We also took time at the early stages of developing this new class of ships to align around a common set of objectives. As we had seen before, people often bring strong but unspoken assumptions to such projects. In fact, they often don't see them as assumptions; rather, they see them as self-evident truths that are so obvious that they don't even need to be said.

Our first task was to get these "self-evident" requirements out on the table for discussion. Then we could have constructive conversations about what our true objectives were or should be.

Our first focus was to design the ship so guests would have smooth and intuitive movement around the ship. This was and is a recurring theme of ours because it is so important. If you are unsure of your surroundings, you will be uncomfortable; if you are uncomfortable, it is hard to have a good time. Easy and intuitive are the first principles of our shipbuilding program.

For the core of the Celebrity ship, instead of a horizontal atrium, the team designed a three-deck-high space—the Grand Plaza—that served as a hub for social activity with bars, restaurants, cafés, and other gathering places. At its center stood the Martini Bar, highlighted by the Chandelier, a stunning lighting feature composed of 765 blades with thousands of LED lights.

I have a personal connection to that bar. Years earlier, at a crew party on an earlier ship, I was assigned the job of serving martinis in the Martini Bar. I liked it so much that the bartenders invited me to do it for the guests on subsequent *Edge* inaugurals. (Of course, the professionals made sure my mixing was up to par. Sadly, nobody offered me any tips.)

The author serving drinks in the Martini Bar on *Celebrity Edge*.

A second goal was to give the ship a stronger connection with the sea and the destinations it visited. We wanted to make it easier to enjoy the sea while shipboard and easier to reach the shore, particularly in destinations where the ship couldn't dock and the guests had to ride a small boat (called a *tender*) to shore.

The solution for getting guests onto a tender boat progressed over a long series of meetings. The normal process is to walk out a small door (called a shell door), literally the size of your closet door, possibly ducking your head to get through, then climb down a rickety ladder into the boat. It was an unpleasant experience. So, the steering committee asked, "What would make a more gracious experience, consistent with our elegant new ship?"

It would need an area inside dedicated to disembarking. Instead of climbing through a small door, we would provide a large opening, and instead of immediately boarding the tender, you would walk out onto a platform that was at sea level, leading to an easy step from that platform onto your launch. It was so easy that you could approach it wearing high heels or elegant evening wear.

Once we had the idea for a platform, the challenge was where to store it. We considered keeping one at each destination, but that would mean constructing and maintaining numerous platforms. Another idea was to leave it attached to the ship, but in rough seas, the platform would stick out, making the ship unseaworthy.

We then explored the idea of a platform you could flip up against the side of the ship like a Murphy bed in a small apartment. However, that platform weighed 90 tons and flipping it up and down was impractical. Moreover, it would be a huge investment to improve a small moment of the guest experience: the tender boarding process. The final nail in the coffin of this idea was that the platform would look like an ugly carbuncle on the side of the ship when not in use.

We decided to look at our two objectives together rather than separately. Maybe we could do something that would accomplish both goals—making it easier to board tenders and connecting the guest experience more intimately with the sea.

The architect devised a novel approach—build a platform as a long, narrow elevator along the side of the ship that could be used at low levels to board a tender and at high levels as a lounge with a view. Because it projected off the ship, it would have views in three directions, offering cocktails, a sea breeze, and a yacht-like feeling of being right above the water. After so many clever but not quite right designs, we finally had a winner.

We initially called the prototype the Magic Carpet, inspired by its ability to glide through the air and transport guests effortlessly. Over time, we realized it was also perfect as the official name of the feature.

Any one of the earlier ideas would have been a dramatic improvement, but the final, transformational design only came about because the steering committee was insatiable. I remember when we finally agreed upon the design one beautiful spring day at the shipyard in St Nazaire, France. There was a large lawn outside our meeting room, and they had marked out the dimensions of the Magic Carpet on the grass; it covered virtually the entire lawn. Harri Kulovaara, Michael Bayley (then president and CEO of Celebrity), and I walked around the layout and were blown away by the size and shape. This new design accomplished all our objectives and did so with grace and style. We knew that we had something that would transform the experience. And it did.

What made *Celebrity Edge* so successful wasn't just the Grand Plaza, the Magic Carpet, or the special attention to detail. It was the way all these elements came together to deliver an experience that was cohesive, intentional, and connected to our vision. Once again, alignment and relentless focus drove us to a great outcome.

It is also worth noting that the final design weighs almost 300 tons. We had rejected the earlier design partially because it weighed 90 tons. It may sound inconsistent, but a "good" 90-ton design wasn't worth the weight; but a transformational 300-ton one absolutely was.

> What makes a project successful isn't just the grand design features. It is the way these elements come together to deliver an experience that is cohesive, intentional, and connected to your vision.

CARESS THE DETAILS

In 2013, when we were finalizing the design of *Celebrity Edge*, our intent was clear: We wanted her to be a dramatic leap forward in cruise ship design. Even the name *Edge* reflected our ambition; we wanted to take innovation and elegance to the cutting edge of modern design.

The previous class of ships for Celebrity, *Solstice* class, had significantly raised the standard for premium cruise ships in terms of both innovation in design and sophistication of décor. With Project Edge, we saw an opportunity to raise the bar even higher.

By 2014, we had finalized essentially all the structural and functional elements of the design, but we had only just begun on the decorative elements. Our goal was to advance the elegance and sophistication of these elements just as we were doing with the structure.

At about that time, Lisa Lutoff-Perlo took over the Celebrity brand as president and CEO. As one of her first priorities, Lisa focused on raising the standard of décor on board *Edge*. We had continued to follow our practice of bringing new blood into every ship design, but Lisa, in partnership with Kelly Gonzalez, took this to a new level and brought in a cadre of new architects whose reputations were among the pinnacle of European designers but who had not previously worked on cruise ships. We had also just completed our CAVE virtual reality simulator, which gave us unprecedented insight into what the finished project would look like.

The result was a tangible upgrade in the level of sophistication and elegance beyond anything normally seen on a premium ship. It was remarkable to see how much of an impact these designers—prodded by Lisa and Kelly's intentionality—made. The color palettes were more nuanced, the spaces more inviting, even the lighting was more comfortable. When I show people around the ship, I love highlighting some of the subtle but powerful details: the elegance of a sculpted ventilation duct, the sensual curvature of a staircase, even the gracefulness of a chiseled ceiling edge. By focusing on the elegance of these design features with commitment and determination, Lisa and Kelly and their teams raised the standard of décor.

I am fond of the quote by Vladimir Nabokov, author of *Lolita*, when he advised writers, "Caress the divine details." I like to think that was what the steering committee did in obsessing over the details to design *Celebrity Edge*. It wasn't just better; it was taken to a new level.

Details matter.

THE WRITING ON THE HANDRAIL

One of my favorite examples of the incredible power of innovation and continuous improvement arose when we were discussing a mundane topic—stairway signs for *Voyager of the Seas*.

The architect presented a sleek, beautiful deck number sign that would be mounted on the wall across from each stair landing. But he complained about one detail—a small braille strip underneath the sign required by our accessibility standards. "It's pointless, even silly," he argued. "How does a one-inch braille strip on a wall 20 feet away help someone who can't even see the massive sign above it?"

This led to a discussion of the Americans with Disabilities Act. Personally, I view the law as one of the most effective and beneficial pieces of legislation I can think of. It requires businesses to make reasonable accommodation for people with disabilities. Obviously, this entails some extra cost for accessibility features, but that cost is minor in comparison to the benefit it provides to the millions of people with infirmities. Yes, there are outlier examples of the law being abused, but in general the law has improved the lives of so many for relatively little cost.

Was this an example of taking a well-intentioned rule too far? We asked the team to figure it out, and they arrived at something really clever. Instead of mounting the braille on the wall across the landing, they proposed putting the strip on the underside of the handrail itself—right where a person would naturally rest their hand. Brilliant. No searching, no guesswork, just put the information where it is needed. It transformed a point of friction into a moment of delight. It was also consistent with our obsession about easy and intuitive navigation around the ship—in this case, for the visually impaired.

The solution showed creativity—what some people would call out-of-the-box thinking. But to me, the more important lesson is that persistence works. The team didn't settle for a "good enough" solution; they kept looking until they arrived at an elegant solution that worked wonderfully for everyone. Today, this simple, elegant solution is used on all Royal Caribbean Group ships.

SUCCESS BREEDS SUCCESS

Success in one effort often leads to a cascade of further successes. I recall being at the shipyard in Finland when the crew arrived at *Oasis* for the first time. Ninety-two percent of the crew had experience on other ships in our fleet, and when they walked on board, their jaws dropped as they recognized the differences. You could see that each one stood a little taller. I have no doubt that the pride they felt in contributing to such an innovative ship was infectious and strengthened our position as the employer of choice.

I saw this phenomenon again when we upgraded the main theater on *Celebrity Apex*. We designed a large thrust stage to bring the actors closer to the audience for a more intimate, immersive experience. (My view was that if a thrust stage was good enough for Shakespeare, it should work for us too.) Complementing the new stage were upgraded sound, light, and mechanical capabilities.

The biggest upgrade was a massive LED video wall 110 feet wide and 28 feet tall. We were all very excited about this wall and what it could do to enhance the experience for our guests. But we did not expect how impactful it would be in enhancing our access to top entertainment talent. Suddenly, the world's top experts in stage design, immersive experiences, kinetic lighting, and other creative arts were knocking on our door for the chance to help create all-new theatrical experiences with state-of-the-art equipment. Suddenly, our ability to attract world-class talent went from *good* to *off the charts*.

During one visit to the shipyard, the entertainment team said they wanted to present to us a short vignette of a show they were currently producing. They had only just gotten access to the theater, but they could present a four-minute run-through to give me a sense of what it would eventually be.

OMG, that four-minute segment was amazing. Of course, when I later saw the full performance, I was floored. But even the four-minute clip got my heart fluttering. The exceptional design of the physical space attracted talent who could make magic. And speaking of magic, the performers in that show worked incredibly hard to make the show special. I'm convinced that if we could power the ship with their energy, we would no longer need to use fossil fuels.

Our commitment to exceptional design led to expanded interest from potential crew, and adding that impressive stage feature increased our ability to book bigger performers. We didn't consider either of those outcomes when we designed the ship, but success breeds success. Alignment and continuous improvement often chain successes one to the next.

ICON OF THE SEAS

One of the most celebrated examples of Royal Caribbean delivering the WOW is the design of *Icon of the Seas*, which had her first voyage in 2024.

The project name—*Icon*—described our aspirations and we also used a new acronym to describe our goal. We decided with our objective to be iconic, the pieces should be "UFB," where U stood for *un-* and B stood for *believable*. Our constant refrain during the design process was to ask whether this ship was "UFB."

It is hard to overstate how successful the Royal Promenade on the *Oasis*-class ships had been. This promenade had transformed the experience for so many and nothing else at sea came close. Our guests loved it—they raved about its beauty and its functionality. They made it clear that it had provided the ship with a true heart, a virtual city center.

The temptation to leave it alone was powerful.

Nevertheless, we knew that, to create something iconic, something UFB, we could not accept that the *Oasis* Royal Promenade was "good enough." We already had the fastest horse on the planet; we didn't want to build a faster one.

Rather, we wanted to make something that was substantively better—something that could accurately be described as "iconic." We struggled for a number of months, and finally landed on a design that would:

- Increase the maximum width of the Promenade from 62 feet to as much as 140 feet
- Add a mezzanine which could include more activities and stretch all the way to the ship's windows
- Make the space more architecturally interesting using the "expansion and contraction" philosophy espoused by Frank Lloyd Wright

With this expanded Royal Promenade, we asked the architect whether there was some novel way to take advantage of the larger footprint and the additional level. After some extensive study, he suggested embellishing the design with a large sphere, called the Pearl, taking inspiration from the library at Tianjin, in China, and the Hayden Planetarium, in New York.

The Pearl would take advantage of all the new features that distinguished this ship from others—the larger footprint, the greater connection to the sea, and the fluidity of the design. It would provide a focal point—something beautiful but unexpected. The Pearl may not have been necessary to make *Icon of the Seas* special, but it certainly made her unforgettable.

The design seemed like it was on track when we were told there was a problem. The problem was the same one that we had faced with so many ships starting with *Sovereign*: The structural engineers disliked what they insisted on calling a hole in the middle of our ships.

In every previous design, we had solved the problem by essentially encasing the opening inside a steel box. But the proposal for *Icon* was to have no box around the promenade, because a metal box would interrupt the views. The space would be completely open in the center for the full width of the ship.

Fortunately, Harri and the Finnish shipyard came up with a solution, an inspired one. Instead of making the Pearl a large spherical object that was inserted into the space, they said, why not use the Pearl as part of the structure? A sphere is one of Nature's strongest shapes. By making the Pearl support the structure, we had a double win—a clever, aesthetically pleasing solution to a complex technical challenge. I particularly like the fact that it feels natural in the space; not something added but something that feels like it was always meant to be.

The Pearl on *Icon of the Seas* with the enormous windows looking out to sea.

The Pearl wasn't just a structural solution; it was a symbol of what's possible when you refuse to settle. The lesson: When the goal is to build something truly iconic, the real breakthrough often comes not from doing more but from doing it differently.

AQUADOME ON *ICON*

The AquaDome was another of the most iconic spaces on board *Icon of the Seas*, but it was not included in the early design for the ship. The AquaTheater on *Oasis*-class ships was an extremely popular and unexpected delight for our guests. It is built around an amazing diving and swimming show that would be outstanding on land but is extraordinary at sea. It was located low down on the stern because it (including all the water) is very heavy.

On *Icon*, we wanted to put an AquaTheater at the top of the ship and all the way forward. We thought the location would be more accessible to the guests and it could become the central focus for a more active entertainment area. It would also need a massive dome to protect our guests and the divers from the elements. Unfortunately, the concern about weight seemed insurmountable. Adding 1 ton of weight on the top of the ship requires almost 10 tons of weight in the bottom for balance. And a dome of that scale would weigh hundreds of tons.

Since a full dome seemed impossible, the early designs called for a much smaller space with a modest dome. But we kept being unimpressed by those early designs. The space was adequate, but only just, and it couldn't contain any of the gee-whiz features we wanted.

We went back to the drawing board and asked Harri and his team and the shipyard to look again at a massive dome that would allow us to have an AquaTheater in this spot. We also wanted to include enough dining and other activities there to make sure the area would be attractive for a wide range of activities throughout the day.

We scheduled a meeting in Miami with all the key players including Michael Bayley (who was now the president and CEO of the Royal Caribbean brand), Harri Kulovaara (our guru of new ships), Jason Liberty (EVP and CFO at the time), the head of the Finnish shipyard, and the yard's technical head. We met in our CAVE, the state-of-the-art design space with its large video monitors and virtual reality simulator.

An early sketch of the AquaDome.

The discussion was animated and productive. Was it possible to put a dome that weighed hundreds of tons on top of this ship? How might such a dome be created in practice? How could it be connected with the rest of the ship so that the traffic flow was easy? Could we live with a half dome in front and a more traditional structure on the back half? (No!) How would we handle the heat load of so much glass? What about the weight of the water; did it really need to be 15 feet deep? (Yes!)

At one point, we decided that we needed a break. We left the high-tech CAVE room to utilize another piece of technology: a coffee machine. But while we gathered around the coffee machine, our discussions continued. With no paper on hand, we resorted to sketching our ideas on a napkin. It felt like a cliché, but in an era where no one carries pencil and paper, we were lucky someone had a pen. By the time we were done, the drawing was barely legible, but it didn't matter; we had a shared vision of what we wanted. We didn't yet know how we were going to build it, but we understood what it needed to be.

An early model of the AquaDome. Note the people for scale.

Afterward, Harri teamed up with the shipyard once again to figure out how to build a dome based on the now-illegible sketch. The engineering was daunting, but Harri is persistent, and the Finns have some amazing engineering skills. Together, they engineered what would become the AquaDome—a breathtaking structure that stands 82 feet tall and spans 164 feet.

I find that, after a while, numbers like that start to lose their meaning. What really brought home the scale of the project for me was hearing about the engineering of one seemingly simple task: how to hoist the completed dome into place atop the ship.

The dome itself is massive, and you can't just hook up a few cables and lift it like a car engine. The structure of the dome had to be kept perfectly level; any deformation of more than three inches across its 32,000-square-foot surface would cause catastrophic damage, shattering many of the custom glass panels.

To accomplish this, they designed a lifting frame, which sits between the crane and the dome. The lifting frame is itself an engineering marvel that took over a year to design and build.

Lifting the final dome into place. Note the lifting frame above the dome.

The lifting frame acted as a rigid cradle, distributing the load evenly while the cranes slowly raised the entire structure with incredible precision. Fortunately, all that preparation was successful, and the entire dome was carefully lifted into place and installed on the ship.

Not a single one of the 600 panes of glass was damaged.

As an aside, Michael Bayley and I had one final disagreement. The highest diving platform on *Oasis* was at 55 feet high, and our shows usually end with some of the divers making that crazy jump. However, the AquaDome only had room for a 49-foot dive. Michael wanted to make a diving platform on *Icon* that was at least one inch higher than on *Oasis*.

Personally, I thought a standard 9-foot dive was already scary, and a 55-foot dive was crazy. We compromised by doing it Michael's way. We added an oculus at the top, which allowed a diver to climb up into a cupula in the dome and dive from a full 55 feet ¼ inch.

Icon of the Seas is a UFB ship that has received widespread acclaim. But to me, *Icon* represents more than that. To me, she represents the latest and most dramatic stage of Royal Caribbean's transition from a cruise company to a vacation company. And Wall Street sees it the same way; the market value of Royal Caribbean is now larger than any airline, hotel chain, or tour operator in America. And more than all the other cruise lines combined.

This vividly demonstrates the value of defining an ambitious goal and having a culture that pursues it relentlessly.

CEMENTING THE STEERING COMMITTEE CULTURE

While the amazing innovative concepts get all the attention, it is also important to focus on the details. The culture needs to applaud not only the grand ideas but also the detailed execution that makes it all possible.

Building that culture and creating alignment around that goal takes the right people and the right commitment of resources. The atrium and its evolution into the Royal Promenade were great concepts, but they would not have succeeded without an obsessive focus on making sure it was comfortable, inviting, and felt proportionate.

To ensure this focus, we created teams responsible for specialized areas of concern. For example, in order to make it easy to get around the ship, the outside of each space should make it obvious what is happening inside. Our guests should be able to understand what is available in each neighborhood without having to read signs or look at maps. It should be intuitive with a casual glance. To make sure this is done properly, we created a Transitions Team to do nothing but look at transition areas between spaces. That sounds extreme, but it results in a more interesting and fluid design.

Many of these concepts are also expensive, and we need to find economies to help pay for them. Again, we set up special teams to look for savings. One, called Weight Watchers, focused on opportunities to reduce the weight of the vessel itself, since weight is very expensive on a ship. Extra weight means the hull has to be larger, the structure expanded, and more energy used to propel the ship through the water.

Other teams included Chief Engineers' Review (chief engineers' double-checking); a team dedicated to Win on Waste (reducing food wastage); Optimus (general cost savings); and Crew Habitat (living quarters, dining, and entertainment for the crew). The point of each of these teams was to approach each topic with an intentionality that could not be achieved as part of an overall design process.

FROM DOUBT TO DELIGHT: REINVENTING ELEVATORS AT SEA

When Julie, our first child, turned five, we bought her a bike. It took me three hours and two scraped knuckles to assemble, and when it was done, there were six parts left over. It was a great bike, but it made a funny noise whenever she leaned left. By my fourth time building a bike, I could assemble it in 30 minutes with no injuries, no excess parts, and no funny noises. The point is that no matter how well prepared we are, nothing provides the same level of confidence as actually doing it.

As we were designing *Icon*, we wanted to use destination dispatch elevators, where you input your floor before you enter the elevator. These smart elevators were faster and more efficient. The technical experts were sure they would be great on the ship. They had installed them in lots of skyscrapers and were confident they would work well on *Icon*.

We weren't so sure. In fact, we were terrified.

So we experimented and experimented. We converted one elevator bank on an existing ship and videoed people using the system. We ran computer simulations. We adjusted the programing. We added signage. Eventually, it seemed ready.

But we were still nervous. No ship had ever had this type of elevator, and most of our guests had never seen one. As a final check, we built

It wasn't the tech that made it special. It was determination and insatiability.

a full-scale mock-up of the entire elevator lobby in our Innovation Lab. The technical people thought this was overkill. They thought our earlier studies were excessive and this was over the top.

But, even after all the early work, the full-scale mock-up taught us things that made it even better. We added additional button panels, reformatted information on the interior panels, changed the shape of the open spaces between floors, and installed additional art pieces in the passageways.

It all worked.

The elevators are even more efficient than we had hoped, reducing average travel time by over 60 percent. Travel blogger Lisa S. raved, "You have to experience it to understand how revolutionary this is." Our objective had been to make sure that the elevators didn't become a traffic flow problem, but the persistence of the team meant that instead of a problem, the elevators became another feature that makes *Icon* special.

Most people will say that it was the use of new, destination dispatch elevators that made the difference. But I know (and now you know) that it was determination and insatiability that made the difference.

WHEN EMOTION OUTWEIGHS METRICS

At Royal Caribbean, we obsess over data to guide every decision we make. But every once in a while, you have an experience that transcends data.

I remember one such moment vividly.

Back in 2010, aboard *Oasis of the Seas*, I was giving my brother-in-law a personal tour. I couldn't wait to show him Central Park—one of my favorite places on the ship, especially in the evening with a gentle breeze. As we strolled the meandering paths, I spoke of the 12,000 plants and trees, the carefully tuned acoustics, how the engineers had solved for sunlight.

I was feeling pretty good about my tour when a man sitting with his wife on one of the benches interrupted me. "You've missed the point," he said, sounding amused. "What are you, some kind of landscaper?" Clearly, he hadn't been impressed with my description.

He went on, "We come here every night. Not for the trees or the engineering. We come because this place is magic. It gives us a sense of wholeness at the end of our day. It is not a grouping of plants and technical stuff; it is a respite . . . a place that speaks to us."

> While data sharpens our vision, it's emotion that gives us purpose.

I had studied all the guest surveys. I had pored over Net Promoter Scores and comment cards. I knew Central Park was a success. But in that moment, talking to a couple who had made it part of their ritual, I felt what the data could never tell me.

I still believe in data. I still study every report. But that encounter reminded me that while data sharpens our vision, it's emotion that gives us purpose.

CULTURE DRIVES INNOVATION, AND INNOVATION DRIVES THE WOW

I am in awe of the innovation that our team drives with every new ship. A staggering amount of effort goes into each new project, each new feature. But that, together with the awesome passion that our crews demonstrate every day, is what delivers the WOW, and delivering the WOW is our raison d'être.

KEY TAKEAWAYS

- Innovation requires more than incremental improvements; it demands a clear, ambitious goal that inspires the team.
- Structured approaches can push teams beyond "good enough" and toward transformational ideas.
- Success comes from a relentless commitment to excellence in both big ideas and small details.
- A WOW is an emotional response. Technical innovation is a means to get there, not the end itself.

Starboard:

The right side of the ship facing forward. From two Old English words, *steor* ("steer") and *bord* ("the side of the ship"). Early ships used a board or oar to steer. Since most people were right-handed, the *steorbord* was always on the right.

Port:

The left side of the ship facing forward. Since *steorbord* was on the right side of the ship, the ship had to dock against its left side to avoid damaging the steering equipment. The left side of the ship was therefore closest to the port. That tradition has even continued with aircraft, most of which load from the port (left) side of the plane today.

Tip: "Port" and "left" both have four letters— a helpful way to remember the difference.

8

Innovation Beyond Ship Design

At Royal Caribbean, it's usually our ships that make the biggest headlines. That makes sense; they're spectacular. People love talking about them and, honestly, so do I. But while so much of the publicity is about our amazing ships, most of my time—and most of our team's time—is spent on things that have nothing to do with steel or design or structure.

Behind every cruise, every smile, every unexpected thrill, there's a world of non-ship-related innovation making it all possible. These innovations create new destinations, streamline the guest experience with technology, design for a more sustainable future, or otherwise enhance the experience.

These efforts aren't sexy, but they are powerful. They grow out of the same culture, the same mindset, and the same principles we've been exploring throughout this book.

ETDBW: THE WEIRD ACRONYM THAT CHANGED SO MUCH

While my suggestion of Project Archimedes was considered too difficult for a project name, ETDBW (which is even harder to remember or pronounce) turned into one of our best. It was not just a name but a rallying cry—something that sparked real alignment across Royal Caribbean.

It all started back in the early 1990s at a meeting with our travel agent advisory board. This was a group of about a dozen standout travel advisors from across the country chosen by our sales team not just for their sales volume but for their creativity and sharp business instincts. They came from a variety of backgrounds, brought different perspectives to the table, and had all built successful businesses from the ground up. Most importantly, each was seen as savvy and articulate.

We'd already had several productive sessions with them before with good feedback and candid dialogue. They got a look behind the curtain at how a cruise line operates, and we got thoughtful suggestions on how to improve. Those meetings were enjoyable and useful but not exactly transformational.

As usual, we prepped carefully. And when we walked into the meeting room at 9:00 a.m., we were looking forward to another pleasant but not earth-shattering session.

What we didn't know was that *they* had also been preparing. The group had convened a premeeting of their own over breakfast at the hotel. And when our head of sales stood up to open the meeting, they cut him off and hijacked the meeting.

"We appreciate everything you've planned," they said, "but we have our own agenda this time." I reacted to this the same way I react every time my wife starts a sentence with "I never told you about this, but . . ."

"We love your product and your people," they said. "But we also want to love how easy you are to do business with, and today, we don't." Booking policies felt like red tape. Communication gaps left people guessing. Our systems required workarounds. The stories came one after another—some big, some small, but all pointing in the same direction.

It felt like someone had just told me that my zipper was down. I was sorry to hear it but was appreciative to have friends who cared enough to tell me something I wouldn't see on my own.

After the meeting, we organized a meeting of our in-house team to discuss what we should do to address their concerns. Everyone agreed that the discussion that morning had been "incredibly helpful." Everyone acknowledged that the advisory board's complaints were justified and that we needed to do better. And then the *but*s started:

". . . but some of their complaints seemed trivial."

". . . but we are a big organization and some problems are inevitable."

". . . but some of our policies are dictated by others, such as credit card companies."

As the internal meeting was drawing to a close, it felt like a business-as-usual conclusion—everyone would return to their normal routine and feel good about a "productive session." Then we would make small, incremental steps to address a few of the specific issues they had raised.

In other words, not much would change.

So, we didn't end the meeting. Instead, we restarted it with a determination to rethink our response. As with the design of new ships, if we wanted transformational change, we couldn't achieve that with a series of incremental improvements.

Once the meeting restarted, we reminded ourselves of the need for true change, and we agreed to approach the issue with intentionality. We all wanted to be *easy to do business with*, and ETDBW became the natural acronym for the effort. Interestingly, the very weirdness of the acronym served to instill it in the organization; it became embarrassing not to be able to recite the expression smoothly and naturally.

🚫 Incrementalism

In the months and years that followed, ETDBW drove meaningful improvements across departments. We simplified contracts. We cleaned up confusing communications. We invested in tools that made booking smoother and faster. And perhaps most importantly, we reminded ourselves—often—that being great partners was just as important as building great ships.

One early commitment we made was to provide immediate confirmation of a booking. In the early 1990s, when electronic access to your bookings hadn't even been imagined, booking errors were common. Even misspellings caused problems; you would be shocked how many ways humans can mess up the spelling of *Smith*.

Mailed confirmations were too slow, so we developed an innovative system to give immediate fax confirmations (remember faxes?). Unfortunately, fax machines were still rare and expensive, so few people had one. We decided that we would provide a free fax machine to our top 1,000 advisors. Each machine cost $600, which was a huge expense for us at the time, but it helped us in our quest for ETDBW.

It may have started as an unscheduled breakfast rebellion, but ETDBW reminds us that sometimes the best innovations aren't the ones you invent; they're the ones that happen when you really listen.

Sometimes the best innovations aren't the ones you invent; they're the ones that happen when you really listen.

EXCALIBUR

Historically, most of our technology expenditures were devoted to automating our internal processes. We spent staggering amounts of money every year on technology, and most went to computer operations and upgrading systems like reservations, accounting, cyber, and so forth. But technology had moved quickly into the hands of consumers. They had become spoiled by providers like Apple, whose tech was so easy to use it felt like magic. And they had begun to demand such magical technology for their cruises.

We had to give it to them, but it was a massive undertaking. The simpler we wanted to make the technology, the greater was the challenge. We decided to call it Project Excalibur for two reasons: First, Excalibur is a strong, uplifting name. It is associated with good feelings and a sense of accomplishment, even a hint of magic. Second, the Excalibur legend is a story of overcoming impossible odds. Using the name Excalibur was intended to reflect that our goal for the project was intentionally ambitious but that—like King Arthur—we would accomplish the seemingly impossible.*

This wasn't just another IT project. In fact, we deliberately kept it separate from IT to avoid that impression (although IT had its own challenging tasks). We set this effort up as an entirely new department reporting directly to me. This was not because I had more expertise than anyone else but because having it report to the CEO gave it a level of importance that ensured that people throughout the company would really focus on it. Project Excalibur was an ambitious undertaking that would be the largest tech investment in our company's history. We needed to do it right.

Project Excalibur was charged with transforming the entire experience, but I will focus here on only one aspect of it. "You never get a second chance to make a good first impression." This expression, often attributed to Oscar Wilde but tracing back as far as Aristotle,

---

* Don't tell anyone, but there was actually a third reason: I love the King Arthur story.

is particularly relevant to one of the most important but unnerving elements of the cruise: check-in.

It is our guests' first physical interaction with our team, but it comes at an awkward moment. The guests have just arrived at the pier. They are in an unfamiliar place in an unfamiliar city. They are a bit disorientated and unsure of their bearings.

On average, this process took about 75 minutes for the cruisers to get from curbside, through the lines, through the check-in counters, and walk up to the ship's gangway. That was too long.

And it took so long not because our process was bad but because of the sheer volume of paperwork required by multiple authorities. Guests had to complete immigration forms for every country on their itinerary, each with its own format. Add to that a security photo (rarely flattering), passport checks, and other steps, and you had a process that was frustrating, repetitive, and boring.

But we were unhappy with the process. It meant that guests arriving on board the ship started out frustrated and tired. Our amazing crew members turned this around quickly, but wouldn't it be great if we could make this experience a WOW instead of an UGH? Couldn't we make a better first impression?

I personally never experienced the issue because whenever I boarded a ship, someone prepared the paperwork for me, and my experience was always as smooth as silk. To learn, I asked the head of pier operations to give me a tutorial using a pretend cruise. I was sure that if I saw the actual paperwork, I would quickly see a few tweaks that would simplify the process dramatically.

Talk about naive. I started to complete the documents for my pretend cruise and quickly got frustrated. The experience convinced me of two things. First, having someone else fill in my paperwork was a great luxury—clearly a perk of the job I had no intention of giving up. Second, we should create a better system to make the embarkation process as smooth for our guests as it was for me.

Our goal needed to be simple and understandable. From the moment a guest steps out of their car to the moment they are enjoying a piña colada on board should be no more than 10 minutes: *from car to bar in 10 minutes.*

For Project Excalibur, our goal was not to improve the check-in process but to eliminate it.

Under the new system, we collected our guests' personal information in advance and had the computer populate it in all the documents needed for the entire voyage. Facial recognition software recognized each guest as they walked through the terminal and sent a green light to the guard. All the guest had to do was show their passport and walk on board—easy-peasy.

And it worked. The system transformed our boarding process. People come on board with excitement and energy, not exhaustion. I liked to watch people's expression as they came through the process. "That's it?" they would say as they started down the gangway. "We don't have to do anything else?"

Excalibur didn't stop at the terminal. It became the foundation for a lot of onboard innovation too. Advanced booking of onboard activities like spa treatments, specialty dining, shore excursions, and shows became one of the most valued (and profitable) capabilities of the system. Guests could adjust the lights, temperature, even the window shades in their cabins—all from one app. With the right touch, the sword smoothly came out of the stone.

We tried some more experimental features too. Luggage tracking? We gave it a shot. Guests could see their bags move from the curbside to their stateroom in real time. It was a neat idea, but it turned out to be too clunky and expensive. The same with using your phone as a room key: Technically, it was cool; in practice, it was a headache.

Still, the core of Excalibur—the reimagined embarkation and seamless digital integration—has been a resounding success. Talk about being ETDBW! It transformed the start of the cruise into something as special as the journey itself. It took an enormous effort, but that effort has paid tremendous dividends both in terms of guest satisfaction and profitability.

In a people business like Royal Caribbean, the system was also a boon to our employees. By transforming the arrival process, Excalibur delivers happy guests on board instead of frustrated ones. By eliminating hassle from onboard activities, Excalibur organizes expectant guests instead of frazzled ones. That enables our crew to perform their magic on a receptive audience rather than a sullen one.

Today, over 95 percent of our guests use the system. When we started, a pier supervisor argued it was unnecessary, saying, "The current system works okay, why spend tens of millions of dollars to fix it?" After the system was in place, our operations head asked, "Can you imagine if we didn't have this today?" That is the power of focusing on the longer term.

MASTERING MUSTERING

The check-in process wasn't the only UGH! at the beginning of a cruise.

By law, every cruise has to start each voyage with a muster drill. This requirement applies to every ship in the world under a United Nations convention called SOLAS (Safety of Life at Sea). During the drill, every person is required to go to their cabin (where their life vest is stored) and then report to their muster station.

As we were designing *Oasis of the Seas*, we wanted to make sure that the stairwells were large enough to handle all the guests on board during an emergency. SOLAS requires a certain amount of square footage of stairwell per person. However, as part of our ABC program (*Above and Beyond Compliance*), we wanted to make sure that in a real-world emergency, this requirement was sufficient.

Using the new digital tools that had recently become available, Harri Kulovaara and his team had a computer model built to simulate an emergency evacuation. The simulation was cool. We could specify the time of day, and the computer would show the traffic flows throughout the ship, with each person represented by a tiny dot.

As cool as the simulation was, it also showed an unexpected problem. At certain times, such as dinnertime, the simulation showed that if an alarm sounded, some guests would be coming from their cabins wearing their life vests, and some would be returning to their cabins to get their vests. When they met in the stairwell, it created a logjam. On the computer screen, the individual red dots converged into a swirling mess. The computer image looked kind of cool—like abstract art—but we understood it could be a problem in an emergency.

We wanted to store the life jackets at the mustering station, but changing the SOLAS requirement would require extensive study, approvals, and time—lots of time. Because the rule seemed so illogical, I asked to see the actual language of SOLAS. I thought, *Maybe, if I read the actual wording, I could spot a way to make an exception.*

The next day, Harri came to me laughing. "You're not going to believe this. It turns out that SOLAS doesn't require the life jackets be kept in the cabins. In fact, the term *stateroom* doesn't even appear in the rules." The practice was simply an old maritime tradition, not a regulatory requirement. And like so many maritime traditions, it took on a life of its own, and everyone assumed it was the rule.

It was eye-opening to me that this tradition—this illogical tradition—held sway over so many professionals for so long. It really demonstrates the importance of never being satisfied, never accepting that something is impossible until it is proven to be impossible.

In the end, the real safety hazard wasn't the size of the stairwell; it was in the failure to question tradition.

MASTERING MUSTERING 2.0

Changing the location of the life jackets was a huge leap forward, but the mustering drill was still a giant UGH! at the beginning of every cruise.

We asked the team to imagine a new way to conduct these drills that would make them less tedious and more informative. They came back with an entirely new format, which we now call Muster 2.0. Everyone still goes through the same training, but now instead of mustering everyone at the same time, each guest watches the safety video on their own, then goes to their muster station at a time of their choosing. It wasn't just about convenience; it was also a safety enhancement.

The US Coast Guard liked the concept and spent more than six months testing it. The tests showed that guests who went through Muster 2.0 were better informed and more engaged. One guest even told us, "I actually paid attention this time—probably because I didn't have to do it while sweating in a crowd." The US Coast Guard approved the procedure, and we had a winner.

On March 3, 2020, the US Patent and Trademark Office issued *US patent number US10582335B1* for "Distributed Muster for Ocean-Going Vessels." We had developed another signature feature that would distinguish the ships of the Royal Caribbean Group.

Unfortunately, 10 days later and before we could implement Muster 2.0, cruising came to a sudden halt due to COVID. As a result, Muster 2.0 ceased to be just another Royal Caribbean innovation and suddenly became a critical health and safety tool. By eliminating the need to congregate in large groups, it made cruising safer and aligned with the new public health norms. And because this was suddenly an industry-wide challenge, we decided to license Muster 2.0 to other cruise lines for free.

We also discovered one fortuitous benefit of Muster 2.0. Under the new system, people went to their muster station when they wanted to, and we didn't need to close the facilities. As a result, Muster 2.0 not only resulted in happier guests but also increased onboard revenue.

LAND HO

I could not be prouder of our ships. They are remarkable feats of imagination, engineering, and design. But they are only part of the overall experience we offer. We were still determined to become a bigger share of the broader vacation market, competing against the likes of Universal Studios, Hilton, and Club Med.

One element of that competition was our private destinations. Our two islands—CocoCay and Labadee—provided an experience that was hard to beat: sun, surf, and barbeques; a Robinson Crusoe experience that you could enjoy without being shipwrecked. Our guests loved them.

But as we entered the second decade of the twenty-first century, we saw a new opportunity. While our private destinations were very popular, they had not significantly changed in 40 years. Our ships had undergone transformational change, but our islands had only undergone incremental improvements. In addition, the growth in the size of these ships gave us the economies of scale that could make substantial investment in the islands financially viable.

Our first big move was to enhance CocoCay by adding a pier to make it an even stronger attraction for our guests. It was a big investment but one we knew would raise the accessibility of the island and enable exciting new developments.

We now had the scale and the opportunity to expand the role of our destinations. We decided to approach this opportunity with intentionality. Just as with new ships, we didn't want anyone to miss what we were doing. We didn't know what we were going to do differently; we just knew it needed to be different—and special.

One day, as I was standing at my desk (minding my own business), I heard a commotion in the hallway connecting the executive offices. I looked down the hall and saw Michael Bayley coming from his office with a boom box playing Queen's "We Will Rock You" and singing (loudly, but out of tune): "We will, we will rock you, rock you."

I had come to expect the unexpected at Royal Caribbean, but this was Michael in overdrive.

He said that he and his team had developed the idea of making the day at CocoCay a perfect day for everyone. He proposed dividing the island in two and "give it a thrill-and-chill vibe." Those who wanted excitement could go to the thrill side, with rides and watersports, and those who wanted quiet relaxation could go to the chill side, with sun loungers and calm pools. He even had a name for it: Project Perfect Day.

It was brilliant. In fact, it was perfect!

We then did what we do best at Royal Caribbean: We brainstormed. We argued. We got excited. We dreamed.

Michael brought the mood down a bit with his estimate that the project could cost as much as $60 million. That was an unfathomable expense—more than we had spent in total over the prior 40 years on our two private destinations combined. But the concept was inspired, and it was critical to our strategic vision of competing in the larger vacation market. We had to do it despite the high cost.

His project name was also inspired. It was not only uplifting, but it also provided a benchmark for the ideas to come. I could imagine the conversation around a proposed feature: "This is Project Perfect Day; is this design perfect?" If the answer was no, you went back to the drawing board.

It was clear that Perfect Day was a great project name, but over time, we realized that it would also be a great name for the destination. And so, Perfect Day at CocoCay was born.

Alignment throughout the organization only comes with total immersion.

We used the steering committee process for the design and were joined by Jason and Harri. This was important, because to achieve transformational change, we needed alignment throughout the organization, all working toward the same goal, and that only comes with total immersion.

The early designs were energizing but disappointing: They showed so much potential, but they didn't go far enough. Each review concluded that much more would be needed to make it "perfect." As we worked through the concepts and reviewed the designs, we gradually had an experience similar to the very first steering committee. We all began to realize that this was not just a great concept; it was an opportunity to create a transformational strategic shift.

However, as with *Sovereign*, there were some who strongly disagreed. They emphasized the fact that our islands were already very popular and argued that dramatic change just wasn't necessary. They pointed out that not only would the project cost a small fortune (they underestimated the final cost, or they wouldn't have said *small* fortune), but it would also take years of development before it could generate any return.

I recall one incident that demonstrated the difficulty clearly. We questioned whether we had enough shade trees given the hot Bahamian sun. The person responsible seemed surprised and responded, "We have planned $6 million in trees, and that was more than we had ever before invested in trees. It is a staggering amount!"

It was telling that his response focused on how much we were spending, not how much shade we were creating. I had no idea how much trees cost (although I learned that they are very expensive to buy, ship, and replant). But I did know that the sun in the Bahamas is strong, and if there wasn't sufficient shade, the day would not be perfect for our guests.

We needed to focus on what we wanted to accomplish, not how the cost differed from past practice.

We went through multiple iterations of the project. It felt like each time we met, we increased the budget by an amount equal to Michael's original guesstimate of $60 million. But each iteration brought us closer to perfection.

When we were done, the thrill side offered the tallest waterslide in North America, the largest wave pool in the Caribbean, and an adventure pool with obstacle courses. On the chill side, we had South Beach with acres of sand and lots of dining options, Coco Beach Club with the first overwater cabanas in the Bahamas, an infinity pool with a dedicated restaurant, and beach areas customized for families, activity, and quiet.

The process of creating Perfect Day at CocoCay was longer and more time consuming than we had hoped (I'm sure that makes us unique). Besides normal delays for design, permitting, etc., we also had to deal with changes in government, logistical issues for an island, and the need to rebuild the island while still operating it.

Building a transformational island paradise is nothing like building a transformational ship, but I was pleasantly surprised by how much our experience with ship design helped in designing Perfect Day at CocoCay. That synergy was exemplified by one junior designer when we were discussing bricks for the pathways.

The architect was explaining why he chose a particular color for the bricks to complement the colors in the surrounding structures. While most of the group was focusing on small differences in tint, one of our transition team designers said, "Excuse me, but I don't think the color of the brick should match their surroundings."

She then went on to say, "The color of the brick should provide visual clues to help people find their way around." This designer was normally part of the ship-design team responsible for transitions and was eager to make it easy to get around Perfect Day just as it is on our ships. The final design did just that and today, when one arrives, the road forks into three paths—a green path going to Chill Island, a blue path leading to the water park, and a yellow brick road leading to South Beach.

Another example of the unique challenges this project encountered related to the overwater cabanas. While we own the island, the waters around us were government property, and they objected to our building structures on their submerged land. After almost a year of discussion, they finally agreed on a creative (dare I say *perfect*) solution: We would still have the cabanas, but they would float rather than be built on stilts. It sounds like a distinction without a difference, but it satisfied the lawyers.

Once construction started, Michael and I visited the island regularly. Each time, we came away more convinced of two things: It would be scarily successful, and it needed more to be perfect. We

An overwater cabana at Perfect Day that even the lawyers love.

needed more and better food offerings, more cabanas and activities, more shade trees.

As our ambitions for the project rose, so too did the costs. We were driven by two competing paranoias: fear that our guests wouldn't value it enough and fear that we were spending too much.

One day, Jason came to see me after a review of the cost estimates. Coming into my office, he said: "These costs take your breath away." A statement like that from your CFO usually makes you take a deep breath. But then he went on to say, "But this project takes your breath away. I'm psyched." We had alignment.

In 2019, after years of preparation and work, the moment of truth approached. During the construction, the work was hidden behind large screens, and few guests understood how massive a construction project was involved. Now, all the screens were coming down, and Perfect Day would be revealed. We held our collective breath waiting for our guests to see what years of thought and preparation and worry had produced.

To use Michael's terminology, it was thrilling and chilling: We were sure they would love it. Really sure. Absolutely sure. But there was this nagging voice in my head that asked, "Are you really, really, really sure?"

As the time came to reveal Perfect Day to the world, we got more and more excited and, simultaneously, more and more nervous. Bookings for cruises with Perfect Day on the itinerary hadn't shown much change. There was no reason they should, but I still looked at them compulsively.

When Perfect Day at CocoCay finally opened, the reaction of our guests was everything we had hoped and dreamed for. The ratings for that first cruise were the highest we had ever received in the history of the company. Demand for any itinerary that included Perfect Day skyrocketed. It became the single highest-rated destination among any of the almost 1,000 destinations Royal Caribbean goes to.

Perfect Day was perfect.

And in my head, I kept hearing, "We will, we will rock you, rock you."

EPIC FAIL IN SPAIN

Throughout this book, I have talked about taking risks to achieve transformational change. Fortunately, most of our transformation efforts were successful, but there have been some notable exceptions. One such example related to our purchase of Spanish cruise operator Pullmantur, toward the end of 2006.

At the time, the economy of Spain was flying high. It had the strongest economic growth in all of Europe and the lowest unemployment, all driven by an amazing real estate boom. One-quarter of all new homes being built in Europe were being constructed in Spain. "Everybody" believed that Spain was on an irresistible upward trajectory.

I bought into that vision (fantasy?) and saw an opportunity to participate in that promising market. We had long and constructive dialogues within the organization and with the board. I pushed for and got alignment to buy Pullmantur at what seemed to be a good price. We completed the acquisition and felt good about the diversification.

Unfortunately, our expectations for the Spanish economy were wildly optimistic. In 2008, soon after we acquired the company, the global financial crisis hit, and economies around the world plummeted. Spain, with its dependence on real estate, suffered even more than most, and unemployment reached 26 percent (comparable to the peak unemployment rate in the US during the Great Depression).

As the economy collapsed, Pullmantur's business was hit hard. In addition, our management approach did not address the problems appropriately. Instead of integrating Pullmantur into Royal Caribbean's structure and culture, we maintained a purely Spanish model, thinking we could recover more quickly that way. That crisis mentality meant that we couldn't realize some of the operational efficiencies and economies of scale that we had counted on.

We struggled to define a winning formula. Despite various efforts, we continued losing money and never unlocked the value we expected. Ultimately, we wrote off $500 million—our single largest write-off—and, during the pandemic, closed the business completely.

The whole endeavor was an unqualified disaster and the single most costly strategic mistake in our history. I try to forget it, but one conversation sticks in my mind. After we announced the closure, I was talking with Eyal Ofer, and he gave me two pieces of advice: First, he said that we needed to learn from our mistake. We shouldn't just announce the write-off and move on; we should make sure we learn from the experience and avoid repeating it. Second, he reminded me that advances don't happen without taking risks. "Don't let this experience suddenly make you timid," he said. "Royal Caribbean has gotten to where it is by being bold and by doing things that have significant risk with significant reward. Don't now only do safe things."

Eyal is always quick with an insightful turn of phrase, and here, he was summarizing sound counsel in two short phrases. His comments were right on both levels; we got this one wrong but not because we took a risk. The real failure was in how we assessed that risk and how we responded under pressure. The lesson was that we should have been more cautious in our assessment of the market and more intentional in our execution of our strategies. We knew that Pullmantur needed to change its market strategy to succeed, but we allowed a fear of the immediate economic crisis to dissuade us from taking the organizational and operational steps that could make it successful.

Fear makes people make mistakes, and we fell into that trap.

ELEVATING MARITIME SAFETY

Starting with the launch of *Oasis* in 2009, Royal Caribbean Group began outfitting all our new builds with an advanced feature: the bridge safety center. This dedicated space is located adjacent to the main bridge and significantly raises the bar for the ship's safety procedures.

Unlike the main bridge, which is primarily focused on navigation, the bridge safety center handles support functions, including communication, emergency response, risk prevention, and guest-related issues. By separating these responsibilities, the safety center reduces distractions for the navigation officer and provides greater role clarity.

In emergency situations, every second counts, and every decision matters. The bridge safety center allows one officer to remain fully focused on the ship's navigation while others manage the emergency. Having a dedicated room (instead of having both functions on the bridge) allows us to eliminate any overlap or distraction between navigation and incident response. It also allows us to organize the equipment and people better for dealing with the incident.

Our early bridge safety centers were relatively simple, but true to our continuous improvement philosophy, we continued to upgrade our equipment and install the latest gee-whiz gadgets. One of the most innovative additions is what we call the *safety table*—a feature born out of a challenge every emergency responder knows well: communication during a crisis.

In any emergency, communication between the bridge, the engine control room, and shoreside headquarters is critical—and notoriously difficult. Traditionally, a mate is assigned to stay on an open phone line, relaying updates between the captain, the engine control room, and Miami's Incident Response Center. This system works, but it's far from ideal—just too much information too quickly.

Enter the safety table, an interactive, synchronized touch table installed in the ship's bridge safety center with an exact duplicate in the engine control room and another duplicate at the Incident Response Center in Miami. All three tables display the same real-time data. If the emergency is a fire, for example, the table might show deck plans with active fire detectors, as well as the location and deployment of firefighting teams. It can even show live video feeds from helmet-mounted cameras on responders.

Focusing on the solution rather than on relaying information drastically improves both response time and the quality of decision-making.

This setup means that everyone involved has immediate access to the same situational information—without relying on messages relayed by telephone. Decision-makers at headquarters no longer need to ask, "What did the captain say about deck 7?" They can see it for themselves, in real time. As a result, conversations become solution-focused rather than information-focused, which drastically improves both response time and the quality of decision-making.

A bridge safety center isn't "necessary." No rule calls for it, and traditional methods work adequately. But intentionality demands that we identify innovation not only in ship design but in every other aspect of what we do. Vessel safety is no exception to the principle that good enough isn't good enough. We should be as insatiable about vessel safety as we are about vessel design.

SMALL THINGS ON A BIG SHIP

I am proud of the big innovations on our ships, but the small things matter too. The same insatiable drive that fuels bold, industry-changing innovations can also push important improvements in seemingly minor details.

Take the Guest Relations desk. It's hardly the most glamorous part of a ship, but it's something most of our guests interact with at some point during their cruise. Traditionally, the desk's design was purely utilitarian—focused on efficiency, dressed up with a bit of décor to make it look nice.

When we built a mock-up of the desk, it quickly became clear that the design created a barrier between the guests and our pursers. It was designed for the pursers' efficiency but paid too little attention to the guests' experience.

With computers, printers, card readers, and extra supplies packed in, the desk had become so large that it felt intimidating and unwelcoming. It reminded me of a police officer wearing all the regulation equipment—necessary, of course, but giving an overall impression of being overloaded and less approachable.

The team redesigned the desk to break down the barriers. They recessed or repositioned the equipment, split the desk into smaller stations instead of one big block, and rounded the sides so that a purser could easily step out and help a guest directly.

No one boards a cruise ship thinking, "Wow, look at how approachable that Guest Relations desk is!" But those subtle details shape how people feel. It's the kind of small improvement no one writes about—yet it makes a real difference. That's the power of never being fully satisfied, and of sweating the little things.

Even on a really big ship.

MORE THAN SHIPS

The same insatiable, innovative spirit that creates such amazing ships also drives incredible paths forward in all aspects of what we do. Royal Caribbean is a cruise company—and so much more. Innovation beyond the ship is about reimagining the entire vacation journey, building a seamless, unforgettable experience that surrounds the guest on land or sea.

My heart sings when I think of all the creativity and persistence our people demonstrate every day, for new ships and for all other aspects of our guests' vacations. As we look to the future, the next big WOW may or may not float, but it will delight.

KEY TAKEAWAYS

- Aligning the entire organization around a clear goal driven by direct customer feedback can lead to meaningful and widespread improvements.
- Understanding and addressing customer pain points is a catalyst for innovation.
- Embracing technology and challenging assumptions can lead to significant breakthroughs.

Quarantine:

From the Italian *quarantena*, meaning "forty." During the fourteenth and fifteenth centuries in Venice, ships arriving from foreign ports were required to anchor for forty days before disembarking in case they carried the plague. The choice of forty days was likely related to Judeo-Christian symbolism: Moses spent forty days on Mount Sinai; Noah's Flood lasted forty days; and Jesus fasted for forty days in the desert.

9

COVID— The End of Cruising?

The call that upended everything came late one night in February 2020: One of our ships had just been denied entrance into Japan. We had been watching the news from China with growing concern, but until now, the problem was limited to China.

Now the contagion of fear was spreading outward from China with port closures, flight cancellations, and border lockdowns. The news became increasingly ominous, and confusion reigned. Navigating all the conflicting messages and requirements became a daily battle. The one thing you need in a crisis is clear leadership and consistency of action. What we got instead was a chaotic patchwork of mixed messages, conflicting orders, and political theater.

COVID-19 began to dominate our lives. Normally, I turn off my phone at night; now, I turned it louder so I could take late night calls from any time zone. Routine decisions became momentous. The torrent of new information and issues was overwhelming. Every day, we were faced with new theories about how to act. Wear masks; don't wear masks. Clean surfaces; don't worry about surfaces. Testing is coming; testing is delayed.

Bookings dropped. Our revenues, which pre-COVID were about $1 billion a month, suddenly began to fall and we were worried that they could plummet fast. If COVID hurt our revenue by 10 percent (as 9/11 had done), that could cost us $100 million a year. And some pessimists were saying it could be even worse than 9/11 (little did we know!).

To preserve our liquidity, Jason Liberty, our CFO, started looking at possible options. When Jason told me that the banks had agreed to a $550 million increase in our revolving credit loan, I was thrilled. I was tempted to ask for his hand in marriage, but both of us were already committed.

We took several steps to protect our revenue. We introduced Cruise with Confidence for guests who were worried about booking a cruise; it allowed them to cancel up to the day before sailing. For the travel advisors, we agreed to pay their commission even if the guest cancelled their sailing due to the crisis.

The White House established a Coronavirus Task Force, and for weeks we had asked to meet with members. Finally, Vice President Pence agreed to meet with industry leaders on Sunday, March 7, in Fort Lauderdale. That morning, he arrived with the CDC director, other administration officials, about 50 journalists, and a phalanx of security. Representing the industry were the CEOs of the three largest cruise lines. In addition, both Florida senators (Marco Rubio and Rick Scott) and Florida's Governor DeSantis joined at our request.

Meeting such a high-powered group was already intimidating, but the vice president also held a press conference beforehand. The atmosphere was chaotic, with reporters shouting questions and jostling for position within the crowded room.

Finally, the reporters were excused, and we started a very constructive session with the vice president and his team. He chaired the discussion with such a formal bearing that—at first—I was afraid he wouldn't effectively lead the discussion. But, as the meeting progressed, he was highly engaged: unequivocal about what he felt was needed but respectful of other views. The two senators and governor were supportive of the industry and encouraged the task force to work constructively towards a proper plan going forward.

At the end of the session, the vice president presented his goals, covered in a velvet glove but with an iron fist poorly hidden. He requested that the cruise industry prepare a plan for enhanced pre-screening of high-risk individuals, expanded testing during the voyage, and clear protocols for handling positive test results.

He gave us a deadline of Tuesday, a mere two days later. This was the precise outcome we had wanted for weeks: clarity—a set of agreements that said, "If this happens, these are the actions we all will take."

We left the meeting hoping that we could agree upon a protocol that would enable us to continue operating while protecting both our guests and the communities they came from. On Tuesday, March 9, we submitted our proposal to the CDC as the vice president had requested.

We never heard back.

On Friday, March 13, we and all the other cruise lines agreed that we should pause all cruises. We thought this voluntary pause would last a month or so.

Cancelling all our cruises worldwide was probably the most difficult and consequential decision I have ever faced. Yet, despite its gravity, the choice wasn't difficult. The disease was spreading rapidly, and any gathering of people posed a serious risk. I was frustrated but knew we were doing the right thing.

But then the CDC did something that took me from frustrated to devastated.

The day after all the cruise lines discontinued operations, the CDC issued a *no-sail* order, ordering us to cease the operations we had ceased the day before. That was fine, but they added a provision that essentially prohibited our crew members from returning home. We had about 40,000 crew members still on our ships, and the CDC order effectively forced them to stay there indefinitely. The order also dictated severe lockdown protocols—much harsher than existed elsewhere in the US or abroad.

REPATRIATING CREW

We did all we could think of to lessen the terrible conditions created by the CDC order. We moved the crew from their cabins to guest staterooms, arranged special meals, provided counseling, and arranged activities, but these things could only lessen a fundamentally appalling situation. And nothing could change the fact that they were thousands of miles from their loved ones.

One of the most humbling and gratifying experiences of my career was seeing how understanding our crew members were. We took regular anonymous polls to help us understand the mood on board, and the polls were far more upbeat than we had any right to expect. There were, of course, some of the 40,000 who blamed us for their misery, but they were a minority. I would have understood if our crew members had screamed at us in rage, but they didn't. Their amazing tolerance made us even more determined to get them home.

Finally, after approximately six weeks, the CDC approved our request to repatriate the crew via chartered flights, but with a set of conditions that were unprecedented in their reach and stringency.

For example, one clause prohibited crew members from removing their masks at any time during the 18-hour flight to Manila—even to drink water or eat. The restriction even applied to the car ride home after landing. Despite our repeated requests for clarification or exceptions, the legal team representing the CDC declined to modify the language.

Our head of human resources expressed concern, saying, "I know the CDC is under immense pressure and I understand these requirements are unlikely to be enforced literally, but why are they there at all?

Surely we can work together to create something that protects people without going to such extremes."

Unfortunately, signing the CDC certificate was just the first step in the process. Even after meeting the CDC requirements, repatriating 40,000 crew members to 90 countries was a crushing logistical challenge. It seemed that every government in the world had issued vastly different rules and regulations for allowing people to come home.

It was an unbelievably complicated jigsaw puzzle, and we assigned the task to one of our strongest executives, Laura Hodges Bethge (who subsequently became head of the Celebrity brand). In our daily meetings, this effort was always our first item of business, but the frustration was so great that tears were common. Every way we turned we seemed to encounter a new impediment. It took a further four months to bring all our crew members home with the last group of six crew members going to Mauritius—the last country to allow its own citizens to return home.

The memory that remains uppermost in my mind is the suffering we saw in our crew—good people trapped for months in quarantine far from home through no fault of their own.

A significant part of the frustration was the disparate treatment our industry was receiving. While our crew members were being treated like superspreaders, nursing homes (with 40 percent of all COVID deaths) had virtually no restrictions. Employees would ask, "How can you, Richard, allow that? Can't you do something?" I asked myself the same question almost every day.

I had no answer. I felt powerless to stop the pain. It was like watching your child get in an accident and feeling that you had failed to protect them. There are no words.

SURVIVING THE PANDEMIC

Our employees began to wonder if there would be a company to work for when the restrictions lifted. Our guests were frustrated to have their holidays cancelled and questioned whether cruising would be possible again. Our travel advisors, many of them small business owners, worried how they were going to stay in business. Our governmental partners were overwhelmed, under pressure, and unsure how to respond to multiple conflicting demands. And we all had children and grandchildren who were confused about their schooling and wondering why the grown-ups were all so frenzied.

People were afraid, and fear makes people stupid.

I had been a reasonably good business student, but Wharton had no course on running a business with no revenue—*literally zero*. The headlines were screaming collapse, and the talking heads on TV were vying with each other to paint a more pessimistic picture of how bad it could be. Our immediate concern was liquidity—making sure that we had enough cash to pay our bills without that $1 billion of revenue coming in each month. And, since no one knew how long the pandemic would last, we could only make guesses about how much cash we would need to raise.

The easiest way to raise cash would be to issue equity—to sell more shares of our stock. Many companies did exactly that, and it gave them a short-term boost. But we felt that selling equity at low prices would fail on both counts: It wouldn't raise much cash (the share price was very low), and it would dilute our existing shareholders. It would feel good for the moment, but be very destructive of value in the future.

We decided that we needed to raise virtually all the money by borrowing based on our confidence that we could repay it when the pandemic ended. And to do that, we had to show our lenders that we could survive even if the pandemic lasted longer than expected. Fear breeds fear, and if some lenders started to worry, it could trigger a stampede for the exit.

The best way to offset such a stampede was to make some grand gesture—something dramatic to show that we understood our cash needs and that we were prepared. We needed to overcome the

> **Fear breeds fear. The best way to offset that fear is to demonstrate we had a plan.**

pressure to panic. We needed to WOW our lenders, to send a clear message: Royal Caribbean is strong and prepared.

Jason had already acted early to increase our revolving-credit facility by $550 million. That gave us a moment to breathe, but only a moment. We calculated that a $2.2 billion loan would give us real breathing room. It would also make clear that Royal Caribbean understood the challenges and had a plan to overcome them—without sacrificing our future.

It wasn't bluster. It was clarity.

And it looked like it would work. Within two weeks, we had financing commitments for $2.0 billion of our goal of $2.2 billion. It was amazing that in this environment of widespread panic our relationship banks chose to believe in us. This incredible support from our lenders reflected the strong relationships that we had developed over many years.

Unfortunately, despite this $2 billion of support, we were still $200 million short of our goal. And, since we had set the goal, our lenders insisted that we achieve it. We had to raise that additional $200 million or the $2 billion was in jeopardy.

In desperation, I turned to two longtime friends, board members, and true believers in the company: Eyal Ofer and Alex Wilhelmsen. Eyal was in England and Alex was in Italy when I called and with the five- and six-hour time difference, it was very late their time. They didn't hesitate. They woke up their people all over the globe, and by the next morning, each committed to $100 million.

Your job is not to panic but to lead.

We were blessed. Their support not only finalized the loan deal, but it also bolstered our credibility to have such a tangible demonstration of confidence from two respected board members. It was a pivotal moment.

It was hard to believe, but it had been only a week since the shutdown. The months that followed were some of the hardest of our lives.

As March 2020 ground slowly into April, many began to fear the worst. We reminded ourselves that our job was not to panic but to lead. Our job was to project conviction and confidence no matter how dire things looked. It turns out that it is incredibly stressful to look like you have no stress. I eat when I'm nervous, and I had to let out my pants twice during this period.

I started making videos in my backyard to try to put some perspective on where we were in the crisis. We had retained some of the country's leading experts to advise us, and they gave us unusually candid advice, which I shared as appropriate.

Another advantage I had was that my family critiqued my performance. I showed my kids drafts of what I wanted to say, and they repeatedly urged me to shorten it. Although I could never trim my talks as short as my kids wanted, my videos would have been even longer without their help.

Vicki Freed, Royal Caribbean's head of sales, started doing weekly "Coffee with Vicki" web sessions with our travel advisors, and thousands tuned in each week. Our government relations team continued to contact government officials throughout the world, preparing them for when we would return. We did large town hall meetings with employees, and each department did smaller versions for themselves.

I also focused on communication with our board of directors. They were ultimately responsible for the direction of the company, and they took that responsibility very seriously. The board had to trust the management, but the management also had to trust the board. Any tentativeness on either side would have been deadly. Fortunately, we had the benefit of many years of working together and that history served us well. It gave management the confidence to listen carefully to the views of directors, and it gave directors the confidence to avoid micromanaging the crisis.

These days, some investors push for shorter tenure for board members based on the assumption that new blood brings new ideas. That sounds nice in theory, but a board without our long and strong history, with their deep knowledge of our company and our people, would not have been nearly as successful. Such a board simply could not have had the confidence and the experience to make the tough choices—especially the focus on the long term—that served us so well during this existential crisis.

Our lead independent director was Bill Kimsey. Bill was the very definition of an *éminence grise* and knew our business well. With his accounting background, he had a naturally cautious orientation. But he also understood and supported our focus on the long-term future. He made sure that we were considering all aspects, but he never tried to usurp a management role.

In response to the crisis, we cut costs where we could, but we approached those conversations differently than after 9/11, when the Survive and Thrive program turned into a Do Anything to Save a Dollar program. Our mantra during COVID was "remember our North Star of emerging from the pandemic strong," and we repeated it emphatically at every opportunity.

We had clarity, and since we had discussed things so extensively, we had alignment. We made thoughtful, balanced decisions like deferring a new reservation system (which was a "nice to have") but proceeding uninterrupted with a new onboard revenue system (which would become an important driver of guest satisfaction and onboard revenue). We also decided to spend money to support our travel advisor partners. For example, when the government announced its Paycheck Protection Program, we started a program to help them get PPP loans. And when the pressure seemed intolerable for many advisors, we made interest-free loans. Cash was tight for us, but it was even tighter for them, and we felt we had to help.

Similarly, many of our crew struggled financially when they got back home. Good jobs were scarce, their relatives were getting sick or dying, their homes were having issues, or their banks were threatening foreclosure. We started an "empathy fund" under the rubric of the RCL Cares program. We did it because we were trying to focus on the long term, and we would need those crew members after the pandemic. Right now, though, it was they who needed us. We allocated

$20 million initially for this purpose and had to raise it several times as the pandemic stretched out. Ultimately, the fund reached $70 million.

Throughout the pandemic, Jason and his team worked constantly with our bankers to raise more money to keep the business afloat. In total, we completed an astonishing 30 financing transactions totaling $36 billion, consisting of $14 billion of new borrowing, $3 billion of equity, and $19 billion of amended loans.

As we dealt with the financial consequences of the pandemic, the hardest thing to focus on was the North Star of our post-pandemic performance. Everyone expressed support for the concept and assured me that they agreed on the importance of that goal. Then the *buts* began:

". . . but Wall Street expects us to reduce the cash drain."

". . . but we have to survive today to get to tomorrow."

". . . but we should never let a crisis go to waste."

The pressure to focus on survival instead of the long term came from every corner—daily calls from the investment community, critical analyses of cost figures, pressure from lenders, etc. The pressure was relentless and always encouraged us to focus on short-term "efficiencies."

Fortunately, the company already had some advantages. Our cost structure entering this period was already excellent. We had taken prudent steps early. Our financing arrangements were tops. Most importantly, we communicated.

You cannot overcommunicate your North Star.

And, unlike after 9/11, we stuck to our guns. We understood that you cannot overcommunicate the North Star. We worked hard to refocus every conversation on where we wanted to be when the pandemic ended.

Clarity is critical to achieving alignment and, as mentioned previously, naming a program and defining its goals can be a big help. To maintain focus within the company, we established a program called Trifecta, with three clear post-pandemic goals:

- $10 EPS (earnings per share), which would be a record for the company.
- ROIC (return on invested capital) in the teens.
- Triple-digit EBITDA (a measure of earnings) per berth.

We knew that many people would not relate to such financial jargon. Terms like EBITDA and EPS are not a big part of most people's daily vocabulary. But the mission was clear. Even if they didn't understand the metrics, they understood the direction. Every decision came back to *"Does this help us to hit Trifecta?"* The targets changed before we went public, but the alignment on the pathway was critical.

THE IMPORTANCE OF CULTURE

Many of the challenges the CDC had to deal with highlight the importance of culture. The CDC is fundamentally a scientific organization that emphasizes research and scientific collaboration. It has made huge contributions in disease prevention, health infrastructure, and health promotion. And it has an impressive track record; its quick and decisive response to cases of Ebola in Texas in 2014 is just one example. The caliber of people with whom we worked at the CDC was exceptional. They are some of the smartest, hardest working, and most caring people I have ever met.

But science is driven by the pursuit of hard facts and is oriented toward making decisions based purely on scientific evidence. Regulatory bodies also rely on evidence, but regulators are trained to consider social, legal, and economic implications as well. A scientific organization can strive to balance such conflicting objectives, but the CDC organization and culture aren't designed for or trained in such a role—especially during a time when the pressures on them were intense and unprecedented. That sometimes led to the kind of confusing compromises and inconsistent advice that the CDC was criticized for.

Science should inform policy, but science can't dictate complex policy choices that require balancing competing objectives.

THE HEALTHY SAIL PANEL

The CDC repeatedly extended the *no-sail* order, and it became clear they would continue doing so indefinitely unless we—not they—created a solution ourselves. We needed more than *permission* to sail. We needed to be sure we had a way to resume sailing safely. The worst outcome would be a rushed reopening followed by an outbreak.

We decided to form an independent panel of esteemed experts to develop rigorous protocols for safe cruising. It had to be seen as honest and credible, a group of people of such depth and breadth of experience that no one could question their scientific or policy conclusions.

We were gratified that Governor Mike Leavitt (former HHS Secretary as well as EPA administrator) and Scott Gottlieb (former Commissioner of the Food and Drug Administration) agreed to cochair the panel. Norwegian Cruise Line had started down the same path and worked with us to develop and sponsor the panel.

Governor Leavitt, however, was trepidatious. He said, "The panel will have to be independent, and you, Richard, can't choose the members or participate in the deliberations." That made me nervous, but the more we talked, the more I saw that he was right. A tough but independent report was better than a supportive but less credible one.

Together, Mike and Scott assembled a team of nine experts in infectious disease, public health, biosecurity, and engineering—a scientific dream team.

The panel met weekly throughout the summer. I was frustrated that it was taking so long, but when I saw how meticulous they were being, I understood. They concluded that the objective should be protocols that would make the risk on board no higher than daily life in your community. That became our mission statement: "If you take a cruise with us, you will be as safe or safer than you would be on Main Street, USA."

On September 21, 2020, the Healthy Sail Panel released a 68-page report with 64 detailed recommendations. They backed that up with thousands of pages of detailed analysis and protocols. And they did so with the imprimatur of a group of such impeccable stature that no one could ignore their conclusions.

The CDC never responded, but elsewhere the report was highly influential, even more impactful than we had hoped. Its recommendations became the framework not only for us, but also for the entire industry.

I know of no other industry, no other company, that went to such lengths. The Healthy Sail Panel wasn't just a strategy; it was a turning point.

PLAN B

Meanwhile, the CDC remained immoveable, and we needed an alternative. Other countries were actively looking for ways that their citizens could safely emerge from isolation. If we could safely resume operations elsewhere, we believed that the CDC would eventually have to accept such a system.

Germany and the Canary Islands said they would allow cruising under strict protocols (based largely on the Healthy Sail Panel recommendations), so we started there with TUI Cruises. Singapore soon followed, welcoming us to resume sailings with similar strict protocols. At the same time, one of our competitors, MSC, also restarted in Italy.

Our experience in Singapore stood out. The authorities were rigorous but collaborative, sharing their concerns and listening to our ideas. Singapore is a strict society, and they monitored every step we took.

The cruises operated without incident, and they seemed as proud of the outcome as we were.

And then, an 83-year-old female passenger tested positive. We braced for the worst, knowing that every other time a case had occurred on board a cruise ship, the authorities had overreacted. Fortunately, the Singapore authorities were thorough but methodical. At the end of a very long day, we jointly verified that there was no spread and no problem for the other guests—just science and process.

Momentum grew. Greece, Israel, Cyprus, and several Caribbean nations reached out asking us to restart cruises from their ports. These were still our cruises—just not sailing from the US. Alaska's senators, frustrated by the economic toll on their state, pressed the CDC and the White House: "You're hurting American workers while safe cruising is happening elsewhere."

The pivotal moment came when we announced that *Adventure of the Seas* would sail from Nassau. The absurdity was impossible to ignore: You could fly to the Bahamas and take a cruise—but not from Miami?

At that point, the pressure became overwhelming and the CDC had to accept it. Plan B had accomplished its mission.

WE'RE BACK!

Finally, the approval came, and on June 26, 2021, *Celebrity Edge* became the first ship to start cruising in US waters since the pandemic started.

I arrived at *Celebrity Edge* in Port Everglades early in the morning the day before departure as the crew was preparing the ship. I came to the pier not knowing what to expect. When I got there, I just looked up and thought about the past year and a half. The ship was clean, her paint looked fresh, and she looked normal . . . just normal. I shouldn't have been surprised, but I was. It was silly, I know, but somehow, I expected that the turmoil of the past year would show on her hull.

I boarded the ship through the crew gangway. It's only about 30 steps from there to the elevator lobby, but on this day, those steps took me an hour and a half. And it was one of the most gratifying 90 minutes of my life.

The security officer at the shell door greeted me with a hug and tears. As we made our way inside, it felt like every crew member wanted to share their pandemic story. There were hugs, tears, and selfies—lots of selfies. Nobody got any work done. We were all too emotional.

Two days later, I repeated that experience with the second cruise ship to resume sailing, *Freedom of the Seas*. It was just as emotional, and, again, I was a wreck. Happy, yes, but also full of pride and a sense of shared purpose. One waiter, his eyes damp but his voice steady, assured me that "the guests who are about to board are going to have the best cruise anyone's ever had."

The guests were equally emotional. I arrived early to the terminal for both sailings, but hundreds of guests came even earlier, eager to not miss a moment. The scene was joyous. Many wore shirts that said, "We're back!" After everything that had happened, they still trusted us with their time, their families, and their dreams.

We were back.

Every company talks about the strength of its human capital, but the resilience and loyalty demonstrated by our employees during this most challenging of circumstances was nothing short of extraordinary. These men and women demonstrated a level of commitment and execution that represents the best traditions on land or sea. They were heroes. Only one word describes them: WOW.

> **The resilience and loyalty demonstrated by our employees during these challenging circumstances were extraordinary.**

I also don't think anyone expected how well the cruising industry would come back financially. We quickly hit our Trifecta goals, and the company has never been more successful.

COVID forced us to rethink everything. But it also reaffirmed what mattered most: our people, our culture, and our purpose. This experience, this horrible experience, proved the importance of culture and how resilient a strong culture can be.

KEY TAKEAWAYS

- Clear, calm leadership and consistent action are crucial during a crisis.

- Taking proactive steps was our lifeline during the pandemic: the Cruise with Confidence program and working tirelessly to secure financing.

- A strategic approach, combined with persistent advocacy, works even in times of crisis.

- Profound human connections and the resilience of employees are essential to recovery from a crisis.

Full steam ahead:

In the era of steam-powered ships, to make a ship go faster, the engineers would open the throttle to generate the maximum amount of steam pressure—full steam. Over time, *full steam ahead* came to be used to symbolize charging ahead with total commitment, momentum, and no looking back.

10

Passing the Torch

As chairman and CEO of the Royal Caribbean Group, I had the best job in the world.

I had the great privilege of working with some of the most brilliant, passionate, and endlessly creative people in the world. These unique (and maybe a bit weird) individuals cared deeply, not just about ships or numbers but about creating WOW experiences for our guests and doing the right thing by our people.

I got to dream big, play with amazing tools, take bold risks, and try new things. I also got to argue—passionately and often—about ideas that I cared about.

Maybe the best part of the job was that I had the incredible freedom to be wrong. I had the freedom to take chances, to stumble, to screw up. Real progress doesn't happen without risk. And being trusted to take those risks without fear of punishment when things go wrong—that's a rare and extraordinary gift that I will forever cherish.

But even the best party doesn't last forever and—after 33 years—it was time to not push my luck. It was time for me to pass the torch to a new leader, but not for the reasons I originally assumed would lead me to this point.

We'd been preparing for this moment for a long time. About once a year, I would say to the board, "I love coming to work every day, but one day, that won't be true. You've put up with me for a long time, but one day, that won't be true, either. We need to make sure that when that day comes, we're prepared."

> Real progress doesn't happen without risk. And being trusted to take those risks without fear of punishment when things go wrong is a rare and extraordinary gift.

In the end, neither reason applied. I still loved my job, and the board still tolerated me. But COVID had changed things. The pandemic was essentially over, but Royal Caribbean would need to restart. It would need a leader who could commit to leading the company through the coming years of exciting growth. At 73 years of age, that was a commitment I was not prepared to make.

Leading an organization of the size, complexity, and sophistication of the Royal Caribbean Group isn't a one-person job. It needs a large and dedicated team of people with the experience, passion, and creativity to maintain and build the culture and to manage an almost unmanageable complexity.

Our commitment to cross-fertilization turned out to be a wonderful advantage in preparing for a transition. That practice provided us with great bench strength. It gave us a pipeline of talented people prepared to move up, most of whom have enjoyed a varied background that prepares them for new or greater responsibility.

Over the last decade, we had methodically worked to ensure that our executives had the kind of experiences that would help prepare them for a new era. For example, Jason spread his wings in several directions. He spent time in Europe virtually living at the shipyard working on our projects there. He oversaw the acquisition of Silversea Cruises and its integration into the Royal Caribbean Group. For a change of pace, we asked him to get experience on another public company board, and he joined the board of a technology company in addition to normal promotions and broadening his responsibilities. The result for Jason and for others was that they became better and broader leaders. This made them better executives in the existing organization but also prepared them to drive further improvements in a new structure.

As part of the transition planning, we also had to consider the automatic shock effect of a CEO transition. If you promote from within, the CEO's old role needs to be filled by another executive, which triggers a cascade of other changes. Filling the role from outside creates a whole different set of disruptions that are at least as impactful. Proper planning doesn't try to prevent the unpreventable; rather, proper preparation takes into account the inevitable turmoil and works to either mitigate it or exploit it.

In my discussions with the board, we decided early on that the new CEO should not be a clone of the current CEO (i.e., me). There is no such thing as a true clone (at least not yet), so looking for a duplicate of a person is a fool's errand. More importantly, the company is constantly evolving. While I may have been the best person for the job when I was CEO (at least in my own mind), the problems and opportunities the company will face over the next 33 years are vastly different and will call for a new type of leadership.

We also made a few specific decisions about process.

One early approach we rejected was asking candidates to present their vision for the future. Such presentations sound good in theory, but we realized that any reasonable candidate would say what they thought the board wanted to hear. A presentation of the candidate's vision would quickly turn into an exercise in pandering.

Likewise, we rejected the temptation to consider whether one choice or another might push certain people to leave. This is always a risk, but we wanted a positive choice of someone who would lead the organization with clarity, power, and grace; we didn't want it to become a defensive decision made to avoid conflict. Happily, turnover throughout the company after Jason became CEO showed no disruption. No commotion, just a collective sense that we were in good hands.

Because we were.

In the end, the transition from me to Jason has been enormously successful. One long-time observer of the industry said to me that he considered it "textbook perfect." Several people have suggested it would make a good business school case study. I believe it has been successful for two reasons:

By far, the most important reason this transition has been so successful is that Jason is an outstanding executive. He's diligent, passionate, and experienced, with a terrific emotional intelligence in an industry where people and relationships matter. Jason and I have worked together for over 20 years. He knows the business, he lives the culture, and he pushes the envelope.

Richard and Jason hiking in North Carolina.

The second reason is that we're good together. A great leader is a necessary condition for success, but it is not a sufficient condition. Ambiguity with the past CEO or, worse, conflict can make any transition difficult.

One of Jason's and my key decisions was what role I would play after stepping down. For my entire working life, I have been an extremely hands-on executive. Could I really let go? Could I resist the temptation to disagree with Jason when (not if) he made decisions that were different from those I would have made?

Fortunately, I understand that clarity is crucial for alignment and that an organization needs to have one leader—and only one leader. I was that leader until January 1, 2022, but on January 2, Jason became that person.

It was important that every person in the organization knew there was a new sheriff in town. And that required Jason and me to act accordingly. I remained as chair of the board, but I did not keep an office at headquarters, and I did not give my opinions to other members of management.

Early in my tenure at Royal Caribbean, we made a decision that was relevant to how I felt my role should be now. At the time, we rotated ship captains on a 4/2 cycle—four months on, two months off. At the end of each captain's vacation, their successor would be in the middle of their duty period, so we would assign the captain to a new ship. This rotated the captains around the fleet, and it meant every ship had a new captain every four months.

Unfortunately, every time the captain changed, there was disruption. It seemed that just as a captain got settled and the crew became comfortable with them, they went on vacation and a new leader took over. This constant changing of the guard meant that the leader (the captain) was not at the helm long enough to drive a common culture.

We decided to go to a 3/3 cycle (three months on, three months off). This meant that every ship now had two captains, one of whom was deemed the senior. Unlike the previous system, the captains always returned to "their" ship. This change was expensive (we needed 33 percent more captains), but it maintained a consistency of leadership that proved effective. Clear leadership is critical to a supportive culture.

The same thinking applied here. Because I was out of the way and Jason knew he was completely in charge, there was room for me to offer suggestions and room for Jason to accept or reject them without feeling threatened. In that way, we preserved the open style of discussion that had served us so well over our 20-year friendship. I do occasionally disagree with him, but our conversations always end with me saying "good luck with that."

It is liberating for him and for me.

One other element that prepared me for retirement was my outside activities. I was brought up in an environment where civic engagement was a given. As I was growing up, friends and family all seemed to be engaged in some way in the community. It was no big deal; it was just what one did.

Throughout my career, I have been fortunate to be involved in many such activities. I am particularly fortunate to live in Miami, where such involvement is welcomed. Retirement has given me the opportunity to be even more active. Early in my career, a friend told me that you should never retire *from* something; you should retire *to* something. Colleen now says I am "failing at retirement" because my calendar is as full today as it was when I was CEO. The difference is that I now choose what goes in my calendar rather than have circumstances dictate it.

What's next for Royal Caribbean? I don't know, but it will be great. We have a world-class CEO, we have amazing people throughout the organization, and, we have a strong and enduring culture that sustains, inspires, and drives transformational change.

I can't wait to see the new heights the team at Royal Caribbean Group will reach and the new WOWs they will produce.

Full steam ahead!

Acknowledgments

First and foremost—and always—I thank Colleen, my wife and co-conspirator: equal parts muse, editor, and co-defendant. She is always there to prop me up and prevent me from falling or failing.

To my children—Julie, Sara, Benjamin, and Jessica—who encouraged me to write this, and then enthusiastically critiqued every page. (Thanks, I think.) More importantly, they reward me every day.

Thanks and kudos to Ed Stephan, whose vision launched this whole wild venture. He created the innovative spirit that so many of us have had the privilege to build upon.

Jason Liberty and the team at Royal Caribbean contributed facts, figures, and memories—and occasionally corrected mine. Their support during my tenure and their continued success sustain and thrill me.

Karen Coffey, my original assistant, one of Royal Caribbean's first employees, and my right hand for over two decades. It's hard to overstate her impact. When the board heard she was retiring, Eyal captured all their feelings with his one-word reaction: "Sell!"

Thanks to Jen Glynn at Greenleaf, the publisher—the folks who turned my Word doc into something that looks and reads like a real book.

Thanks also to Greg Lichtenberg, whose collaboration proved that two heads can be better than one—and whose fingerprints are nowhere and everywhere.

Mark Fortier, my publicist—because even books need a hype man, and he was so much more than that.

And to the many others—colleagues, friends, and quiet heroes—who offered advice, lifted my spirits, or simply showed up at the right moment: thank you. Your help mattered. If your name isn't here, it's only because there weren't enough pages to fit all the people I owe.

As for the inevitable errors, omissions, and bad ideas—I alone am responsible. The rest of them tried to warn me.

It's the people, it's the people, it's the people.

Glossary

STRATEGIC PILLARS

Above and Beyond Compliance (ABC): Going beyond minimum regulatory requirements to achieve higher standards, particularly in environmental and safety areas.

Alignment: The state where team members rally behind a shared vision or plan, even when it's not their personal preference, going beyond mere consensus.

Continuous improvement: The permanent mindset of constantly seeking better ways to accomplish tasks, aspiring to be better than yesterday and even better tomorrow.

Cross-fertilization: The practice of moving employees across different departments to broaden their perspective, break down silos, and inspire fresh thinking.

Delivering the WOW: The central philosophy that prioritizes creating extraordinary experiences that exceed expectations for guests and employees, serving as both a rallying cry and cultural touchstone.

Intentionality: The focused, disciplined approach that ensures every step taken aligns with longer-term goals without shortcuts or easy compromises.

North Star: The guiding principle or long-term vision that aligns all company decisions and actions, providing clear direction even during challenging times.

Rule of thirds: The framework requiring new projects to be "one-third traditional, one-third evolutionary, and one-third revolutionary" to balance innovation with guest comfort.

Skate to where the puck will be: Making decisions based on future trends rather than current conditions, inspired by Wayne Gretzky's hockey strategy.

Survive and thrive: A dual-focused approach to crisis management that balances short-term survival with preparation for future success.

CULTURAL DRIVERS

Caressing the divine details: The practice of obsessing over seemingly minor elements that collectively create an exceptional guest experience.

Charrette: A collaborative working group discussing and refining design, inspired by the French Beaux-Arts school tradition of collaborative improvement.

Democratizing the process: Encouraging design and decision-making input from people across the organization regardless of their specialized knowledge.

Employer of choice: The strategic goal of being the preferred employer in the industry, to attract and retain the best talent.

GOLD Anchor Standards: A behavioral framework for crew members: Greet the guest, own the problem, look the part, and deliver the WOW.

It's the people, it's the people, it's the people: A mantra emphasizing that employees are the foundation of company culture and success.

UFB (Un-f*ing believable): An internal standard for innovation that pushes beyond conventional expectations to create truly astonishing experiences.

OPERATIONAL APPROACHES

Double-Double: Our 2015 program targeting the doubling of earnings per share (EPS) and achieving double-digit return on invested capital (ROIC) within a defined timeframe.

ETDBW (easy to do business with): Our 1990s company-wide initiative to reduce friction points for travel advisors and partners.

Trifecta: Our three-pronged post-pandemic recovery framework with specific financial targets to align organizational efforts.

LEADERSHIP PRINCIPLES

Clarity is crucial for alignment: The principle that clear communication and expectations are essential for organizational unity.

Fit over fault: An approach to personnel changes that prioritizes compatibility with the team and culture over assigning blame.

Good enough isn't good enough: A commitment to excellence that rejects mediocrity and pushes for exceptional standards.

Everyone gets their say; not everyone gets their way: A principle for inclusive decision-making that balances input with decisive leadership.

What gets measured gets better: The principle that tracking performance metrics inherently improves performance.

You never get a second chance to make a good first impression: A focus on optimizing guests' initial interactions with the company.

Author photograph by Malena Vasquez Studio

About the Author

RICHARD FAIN is chairman of Royal Caribbean Group. He served as chairman and CEO from 1988 to 2022 when he transitioned to his current role as chairman. Under his leadership, the company grew from a small cruise line to its current place as one of the world's most valuable vacation companies.

Recognized for his "visionary leadership," Mr. Fain was named one of the thirty World's Best CEOs by *Barron's* three years running and received the Ultimate CEO Award from the *South Florida Business Journal*. His international awards include the rank of *Officier in the Légion d'Honneur* of France and Commander, First Class, of the Order of the Lion of Finland.

He and his wife of fifty-six years have four children and eight extraordinary grandchildren.